TO BAGHDAD AND BEYOND:
HOW I GOT BORN AGAIN
IN BABYLON

JONATHAN WILSON-HARTGROVE

Cascade Books
A division of Wipf & Stock Publishers
199 West 8th Avenue, Suite 3 • Eugene OR 97401

Cascade Books
A division of Wipf & Stock Publishers
199 West 8th Avenue, Suite 3
Eugene, OR 97401

10   9   8   7   6   5   4   3   2   1

*For Leah, my traveling companion
to Baghdad and beyond,
and Jim, who has shown us the Way.*

TABLE OF CONTENTS

PREFACE

When Christians in the early church read the book of Revelation, they understood its symbolism. They realized that Babylon, the wicked city described in the latter part of this book, referred to the dominant societal system in which they lived. It referred to the Roman Empire.

As contemporary American Christians read the book of Revelation within the dominant societal system in which we live, we must ask ourselves whether or not our own nation-state has become the modern equivalent of the Roman Empire. We must ask, "Has America become Babylon?" That is the question that Jonathan Wilson-Hartgrove, the author of this book, endeavors to answer.

In Revelation 17:5, Babylon is described as "The Great Whore." She is viewed as a societal system that seduces people into worshiping her by offering them an array of alluring consumer goods that they find irresistible. According to what we read in chapters 17–19 of the book of Revelation, the merchants who participate in the economy of Babylon grow rich as they profit from the sale of these things. It is of no consequence to these merchants that they are profiteering in a global economy that is contingent on the exploitive exhaustion of natural resources (see Rev. 18:3, 12–13). The wealth that they gain is all that matters.

To the dismay of all who live in Babylon, the day comes when the

Empire falls. From that day, the merchants weep because the economic benefits that Babylon provided for them are no more. The industries of Babylon close down; and the music that once blared through its streets is heard no more (Rev. 18:22). Alas, Babylon is no more, and those who worshiped Babylon weep.

But there is another reaction to Babylon's fall. It is the celebration of the angelic hosts. They cheer because the violence on which the empire depended for maintaining its powerful hegemony over the earth is ended. The bloodshed necessitated by its social policies is ended (Rev. 19:1–3). For all of this the angels shout, "Alleluia!"

Is this what will happen to America? Will ours, the only standing superpower in the world today, one day collapse? Is this apocalypse a foretelling of our national destiny?

Babylon, in the imagination of Israel, was once the city of Nineveh, the city referred to in the book of Jonah. But the difference between Nineveh and Babylon is notable. When confronted with its sinful ways, Nineveh repented and thus, escaped the fate of its successor. Is it possible that America, like Nineveh, might repent? Is it possible that our nation could change its ways? And if such repentance was to occur, would we not all have to undergo a spiritual conversion that would enable us to see ourselves and the rest of the world through new eyes?

This book is about a young couple who left the comforts and joys of university life to make a journey to Iraq and in making that journey underwent a "born again" experience. It is the story of Jonathan and Leah Wilson-Hartgrove and their bold adventure of faith when they, as Christian peacemakers, traveled into Iraq just as the second Gulf War was getting underway. As you read their story, you will be challenged to rethink your own views about war—not just this war, but any war. You will be led to ask if being Christian requires following the clear admonitions of Jesus to love our enemies and obey the biblical mandate to overcome evil with good. In the end, you will likely ask yourself whether the Jesus who told all of his followers to put up the sword lest they die by the sword, trumps all those theologians, from St. Augustine to John Calvin, who argued a "just war."

These young people do not simply call us back to the Christianity of the Sermon on the Mount; they model for us some possible ways to create alternatives to Babylon. They tell us how new communities of faith, marked by Christian hospitality and monastic discipline, are growing up in places across America. They are offering a countercultural way of life that heralds something about the coming Kingdom of God.

In the closing chapters of the book of Revelation, we not only read about Babylon, but we also read about another city. It is the New Jerusalem!

When the Christians in the first century read about the New Jerusalem, they knew that it represented the new humanity that was being created by the resurrected Christ. They understood that this New Jerusalem was the church. This young couple is asking whether we are willing to become part of this alternative society or whether we will continue to be part of an acculturated ecclesia that is comfortable in Babylon and legitimates its way of life. It is the ultimate question about our historical destiny and it is asked and somewhat answered in the existential struggles of the brave young couple you will read about in the pages ahead.

Tony Campolo
Professor Emeritus
Eastern University
St. Davids, Pennsylvania

INTRODUCTION

YE MUST BE BORN AGAIN

Where I come from, nothing is more important in life than getting born again. "Except a man be born again," Jesus said, "he
cannot see the kingdom of God." We like that verse in King, North
Carolina. At the root of all our problems, be they personal, family,
social, or political, lies sin. The Scriptures teach us that all have sinned
and so inherited this sickness that leads to death. Everybody dies.
There's no escaping it. The only way out is to give your life to Jesus—
to die to sin and be resurrected with Christ into new life. Where I
come from, you must be born again.

I know a man in my home church who can hardly talk to anyone
for more than five minutes without telling the story of how Jesus saved
him in 1977. It's just that important to him. Nothing is more memo-
rable than the day he was born again. I remember my own experience
like it was yesterday. It was a Sunday evening in July at the Mt. Olive
Baptist Church. Andy Oliver, our youth minister, was preaching, and
while I don't remember much of what he said, I do remember leaning
over to my dad and telling him that I wanted to go forward during the
altar call. "That's wonderful," Dad said. "Come on, I'll go with you."

"But I can't," I said with some embarrassment. Andy's sermon had
moved me inside, but I wasn't moving from that pew. As the organist

finished playing "Just As I Am," I felt like everyone in the room was looking at me. I slipped out quickly when the song had ended and went home to play with my brother and our friend David. Later that night Mom and Dad called me upstairs to tell me they were proud of my decision. If I wanted, they said, I could meet with Andy and talk more about how I was feeling. I agreed; they made the call. One day after school that next week Andy stopped by the house, picked me up, and took me to the church. He asked if I'd like something to drink, poured a glass of water in the kitchen, and then pretended to spill it on me as he returned to his desk. (He'd filled the glass with little pieces of paper towel as I was listening to the water running.) I laughed, and the ice was broken.

Andy asked me to explain what I thought it meant to give my life to Jesus. I did, and he said he thought I understood it as much as anyone did. We talked with Preacher Yates about baptism, set a date, and that was that. Most of my family came that Sunday to see me go down into the baptismal waters. After he'd pulled me back up, Preacher Yates said the old man had been washed away and I was a new man inside. At seven years old, I was delighted to be called a man. And with that, I was born again.

The Christian music artist Rich Mullins used to say that when he was in high school he got born again once a year on the last day of summer camp. When he got to college, he realized he was so messed up that he needed to get born again every couple of months. "The more I live," Rich said close to the end of his life, "the more I believe that I need to be born again every day." I think Rich was on to something. Jesus said that anyone who would be his disciple would have to take up her cross daily and follow him. To take up a cross, as his first century audience understood, was to die. But if we are to die daily, doesn't that mean we might have to be born again every day as well? Maybe Rich was right in suggesting that we need to get born again more than once.

This book is about how I got born again in Babylon. And I should warn you: it happened more than once. Babylon, historians tell us, was once upon a time the land we now call Iraq. At the beginning of the second Gulf War, my wife, Leah, and I traveled to Iraq with the

Christian Peacemaker Teams as part of a delegation whose mission was to offer a ministry of presence and witness the effects of war. This book tells the story of how I was born again on that short trip. It is also, however, the story of how I came to see that we who live in America also live in Babylon. Babylon is not only the land now known as Iraq. It is also, in the language of our own time, the "last remaining superpower." As my teacher, Tony Campolo, likes to say, "America may be the best Babylon there has ever been, but she's still Babylon." The conversion I've experienced on U.S. soil before and after Baghdad, then, has been as important in the renewal of my mind as our experience under the bombs in Iraq. *To Baghdad and Beyond* is a testimony about the work of regeneration that the Holy Spirit is doing in one young Christian's life.

At the same time, this is also a story about the evangelical church in North America today. I write as one shaped by the spirit and institutions of evangelicalism, eager to follow Jesus, but convinced that we in the American church face a crisis. Our time in Iraq opened my eyes to a new movement in the North American church—a return to the radical "third way" that Jesus offered the people of his own day. This book is an attempt to articulate that vision in brief. The best way I know to describe this vision of God's "third way" is to tell my own story: how I came to see this vision, why it took me to Baghdad, and how my own life (and the lives of others) has been changed. Mine is, of course, only one story. What follows is neither an objective study of the options that stand before the church in America today nor a systematic presentation of my own "agenda." It is a modest attempt to tell the truth about what has happened to me. My hope is that such a testimony will excite others with a passion so compelling that they'll want to follow the Way of Jesus in the concrete reality of the twenty-first century world. Dietrich Bonhoeffer, the German theologian who resisted Hilter's regime in Nazi Germany, says this better than I can:

> All I have done is to jot down as they come to me some of the discoveries made by a circle of like-minded friends, discoveries about the business of human life. The only connection between them is that of concrete experience. There is nothing new or

3

startling about them, for they have been known long before. But to us has been granted the privilege of learning them anew by first-hand experience.

My "circle of like-minded friends" is an ecumenical collection of evangelicals, Anabaptists, Catholics, and Mainliners. We have begun in the past year to refer to the Way that Jesus is revealing to us as a "new monasticism." It is "monastic" in that it does not lead us to the centers of power but out, like the Desert Fathers and Mothers, into the abandoned places of Empire, where only God can save us. It is "new" in that we do not see our rule of life as a special vocation for "super Christians," but as a viable Way for the whole people of God— male or female, married or single, ordained or not. In June of 2004, we gathered for what we hope will be the first of many "Schools of Conversion" where we talk and pray together about faithfulness in discipleship. Without the encouragement and prodding that has come from this circle, I could not be who I am and this book would not have been possible. I'm especially happy that both my parents and my parents-in-law are part of this group. I am, of course, who I am because of who they are.

My "inner-circle" is the community I live with at Rutba House, a house of hospitality, peacemaking, and discipleship in the Walltown neighborhood of Durham, North Carolina. We submit ourselves to the spiritual and practical direction of Chapel Hill Mennonite Fellowship and the local churches of Walltown Neighborhood Ministries. Together with these folks—and often through them—I get to witness God's work day by day. I believe in the vision this book articulates partly because I get to see glimpses of it firsthand. For the record: we screw up often. The grace of forgiveness, though, is one of the most beautiful gifts I have known in community. I could not write a book like this anywhere else. Rutba House is indeed a gift. Thanks to Isaac, Ronnie, Roy, Julie, Alvin, Sarah, our neighbors in Walltown, and all the wonderful guests who've passed through the Rutba House.

Finally, I'm grateful for Leah who is my partner in this school of discipleship called marriage. From her I have learned who I am, more so than from any other human being. Because of the stability that her faithfulness provides, I am able to do things I would have never done on my own. Going to Baghdad, for example, is something we're both convinced we could have only done together. People who read our reports from Iraq via e-mail noted the personal tone of Leah's writing alongside the more abstract and objective tone of mine. If the story that follows is in any way authentic, it is because I've learned from Leah some of what it means to be real. She is a patient teacher of the wisdom that it's not enough to know the right answers; you must be born again.

I.

WHEN GOD CALLS

It was usually on Sunday evenings in the summer that the missionaries would come to visit Mt. Olive Baptist Church. We almost always had a church supper, usually potluck (though once I remember the missionaries from Gaza fixing an authentic Middle Eastern meal; it was the first time I ever tasted hummus). After the meal, there was time for story-telling and slide shows. Over the hum of a slide projector fan, the missionaries would tell us stories about what God was doing in Ghana and Honduras and Bangladesh. When I got home afterwards, I always got out the globe that my parents had given me and traced a line from North Carolina to the places I'd just learned about. My young imagination was left to wonder whether God would ever call me to make such epic journeys of faith.

Those Sunday evening visits from mysterious men in short-sleeved dress shirts and women who could sing in Chinese are my earliest memories of a sense that the Christian life is an adventure. In King, North Carolina, there was nothing particularly adventuresome about going to church. The real radical thing would have been choosing *not* to go. (My older brother flirted with this expression of independence in our teenage years, but he was always more courageous than I.) Though we were Baptists, believing that people join the church by a personal confession of Christ, the fact of the matter was that Christianity had become socially acceptable. It was the norm. Jesus was, no doubt, a great comfort and sustaining power to the saints at Mt. Olive who labored faithfully to "do the work of their hands"—plow the fields, keep house, raise kids, and foster a healthy community. The call to costly discipleship, though, was a message the missionaries brought.

I remember one missionary in particular who sang a humorous song entitled "Please Don't Send Me to Africa!" during his presentation. "Please don't send me to Africa / Where there are lions and tigers and bears," he sang. This was the prayer he had prayed when he first sensed God's call on his life. In a clever rhyme that I've since forgotten, he sang about how he had been willing to do anything God wanted *except go to Africa*. Finally, of course, God called him to Africa. He served as a missionary there for some thirty years. His was a Jonah story: the reluctant messenger is called to preach in a foreign land. Despite resistance, he goes. What follows is an adventure. It was an Abraham story: a simple believer is called to go to a place that God will show him. What he must do is trust and go. The rest is history—the history of the people of God. It was a gospel story: "follow me," Jesus says to his disciples. And despite all their questions and reasons for resistance, they follow. When God calls, the missionaries taught me, you follow. The adventure that follows is life in the kingdom of God.

So it was that I sat my parents down at the kitchen table when I was fifteen years old and told them I felt God calling me to spend the next summer in Africa. I'd found an ad in a Christian magazine for an organization called "Teen Missions" that trained teams of young people in Bible, evangelism, and basic construction and sent them around the world to do summer mission projects. Teen Missions was starting a new "Desert Angels" team that would ride dirt bikes through the countryside of Zimbabwe, show the "Jesus" film in small villages, and help construct a home for AIDS orphans. After some discussion about the details of this adventure, my parents agreed that the missionaries were right: when God calls, you follow. I set out the next June for the "Lord's Boot Camp" in Merrit Island, Florida.

Teen Missions was serious about preparation. They woke us up at 6:00 a.m. every morning to run an obstacle course through a Florida

7

swamp, stacking cinder blocks with Bible books written on them in order, climbing Mt. Zion (a pile of thousands of old car tires), swinging on a rope across the "Slough of Despond," and finally getting every member of our team over a twelve foot wall. All of this before 6:30 a.m. They taught us to spend time alone, reading the Bible and praying in the early morning. We had to recite memory verses before each meal, giving new meaning to Paul's admonition, "He who does not work does not eat." They taught us to work hard, "as if unto the Lord," whether we were learning to lay brick or washing our clothes in five gallon buckets. As we did it all, we sang.

Africa was easier than boot camp. I think Teen Missions meant it to be that way. We took a cargo truck from the airport in Johannesburg to a little mission in southwestern Zimbabwe. There were no windows in the truck, but we knew we had turned onto dirt roads by the dust that filled the air. Finally, we stopped, and someone opened the rollaway door at the end of the truck. I looked out into a new world, wider than my imagination and every bit as mysterious as the stories I'd heard from our missionary visitors in King. What I was seeing, I knew, would change me. It was an opening, I thought. The horizon looked more expansive than ever. My soul swelled. Where might I go from here? The possibilities were endless. To a sixteen-year-old kid from rural North Carolina, that thought was exciting.

I did not even go back home before setting off on my next adventure. My best friend, Marty, met me at the airport in Miami on my way back from Zimbabwe, and we flew together to Venezuela. I felt like quite the world traveler. We had gotten special permission to miss the first week of school back home so we could help out with two weeks of summer camp for poor kids from the city in Venezuela. It felt wonderful to be together with Marty on this epic journey I thought God was leading me on. We played with kids all day and sat up late at night talking about Jesus and our lives, dreaming about the possibilities that lay before us. Life was so exciting we hardly even needed to sleep.

One day when we were eating a lunch of refried beans and tortillas and drinking iced coffee, the missionary we were working with brought me a cell phone and told me my father needed to ask me a question. Senator Strom Thurmond's office had just called, Dad said, and wanted to know if I'd like to come to Washington, DC, in two weeks and take the Senate Page position I'd applied for. "Of course!" I said. "Are you sure you want to be away from home even longer?" Dad asked. I made no hesitation assuring him that it would be just fine. I could not have been more excited. From Africa to South America to Capitol Hill—my head was spinning as I packed my bags and headed home for a few days. This following Jesus was more fun than I'd ever anticipated.

Our pastor invited Marty and me to share about our summer at the Sunday night service after we got home. I was eager to do so. After three months of getting up early every morning to read the Bible, I felt like I had a lot to say about God's call on our lives as Christians. Best I remember, I didn't talk about Zimbabwe or Venezuela very much. What I was really excited about were stories from the Bible about Abraham and Moses and Caleb. I'd learned that *Caleb* means "dog" in Hebrew, and I preached that he was a bulldog for God, stubbornly determined to follow the Lord and lay claim to his promises. After a few months on the "mission field," I'd returned to preach the same sermon that all those missionaries had proclaimed to me over the years: when God calls, you have to follow.

Going to DC seemed to be the next step on my journey. A summer of mission work had exposed me to the problems of the Third World. In Africa we had met some of the AIDS orphans that would be living in the four-room house we were building. We heard how their parents had died and aunts and uncles had adopted them; but now the aunts and uncles were dying. It was clear that the problem was much bigger than our small attempt to help. The orphanage would be full even before we got it finished. In Venezuela I was introduced to the *barrios*—slum neighborhoods that surround the cities of Central and South America. Attracted by the possibility of work in the city, millions of people lived in shacks on the hillsides surrounding Caracas. At night the fires they lit to cook by produced a shimmering display of star-like lights that were deceptively beautiful. By day we saw the filth of grinding poverty. These "global" issues that I had just been exposed to were clearly political problems. They were a world away from life in King, North Carolina. They were, however, just the sorts of things that people inside the loop of Washington talked about. As I wondered what the

Lord was calling me to for my life's work, I began to dream of the possibility of being a Christian statesman.

One of the reasons I had applied for a Senate Page position in the first place was the suggestion from a U.S. Naval Academy cadet that a letter of recommendation from a Senator was the best way to get into the Academy. And the Academy, I had learned, was a fine way to get into politics. My parents had always told me that finances were tight, so I should work hard for scholarships that would make it possible to go to college. When this cadet visited our school and talked about the rigorous academics and disciplined life at the Naval Academy, I got excited. About that same time, a four-star general from King retired from the Pentagon and returned home to a parade down Main Street celebrating his service to our country. That next Sunday, he worshiped with us at Mt. Olive. We all stood to applaud him, and the pastor lifted him up as an example to all of us of what it could mean to serve God and country honorably. Though I hadn't connected all of the pieces at the time, they started to come together in my mind as I traveled to Washington. The page position might turn into a recommendation that could turn into an education at the Naval Academy that would lead into a short military career that would be a wonderful springboard to a career in politics. My summer travels had added a new question: perhaps God was calling me to this, preparing me to be one who would stand for justice in the world's greatest center of power. If God called, was I ready to follow?

The rigorous schedule of life on the Hill in DC tested my new discipline of early morning prayer. From 6:00 to 9:00 a.m. I completed my school assignments for the day before walking over to the Senate's Russell building, where I worked from 9:00 to 5:00 p.m. Still, I got up each morning at 4:30 to read the Bible and ask God to speak to me. I was eager to hear his call. At that time, Dr. Lloyd John Ogilvie was chaplain of the Senate and led a Bible study once a week during the lunch break. I went every week I was in Washington. That I went, however, was a strange thing to most of the folks in Senator Thurmond's office. Often, they worked straight through their lunch breaks. If they took one, though, they couldn't imagine reading the Bible as a very good use of their time. Whatever the possibility of doing the Lord's work in Washington, I began to suspect that it wasn't the first thing on most people's minds.

In his reflections on the book of Philippians that September, Dr. Ogilvie would often tell stories about his pastoral work in the Senate. One day he told us about a young page who was leaving the Senate after his term. "I'll be back," the young man had said to Dr. Ogilvie. "Only next time, I'll have a seat on the Senate floor." This young man in Dr. Ogilvie's story could have been me. I waited to hear his response: " 'Just don't let it cost you your soul,' I told the young man." Dr. Ogilvie paused. "Just don't let it cost you your soul." There was a sadness in his words that began to settle onto me as I thought about them. My epic journey of following God had been so exciting up until that point that I hadn't stopped to think that all of this could cost someone his soul. The feeling of excitement I had was not enough to ensure that I was doing the will of God. Nor was the fact that I said I was following God. A great number of people—the Pharisees chief among them—had done terrible things in the name of God. Dr. Ogilvie's word of caution set off a string of questions. Was it possible to serve God in Washington? Who seemed to be doing that well? How pure were my own motives? Was my attraction to politics really about helping the people I had met in Zimbabwe and Venezuela, or was it about getting the sort of recognition that four-star general had received in King? And if I really cared about the poor of the world, was Washington the place to go to help them? I was confused. After office hours, I walked the streets of Washington asking God (and myself) these questions.

For dinner I would usually stop at Union Station where there was an assortment of restaurants in the basement. On my way in one day I heard a man ask me, "Could you spare some change?" I looked straight at him and kept walking without saying a word. I remembered what folks in King had said about panhandlers in the city—how they're mostly drunks and drug addicts who need to learn to help themselves. Then one of my memory verses from the summer came back to me: "When you did it to the least of these, you did it unto me." Had I just ignored Jesus at the front door of Union Station? Or was the fellow I stared at in silence just another drunk? If he were Jesus, I thought, it'd be good to give him what he asked for. If he were just another drunk, well, he probably needed to meet Jesus. So I went back to my room. There I had a box full of Billy Graham tracts that my church had given me with questions like, "Where is God When it Hurts?" on the front. I also had in my drawer a couple hundred dollars that my parents had given me to buy food and do my laundry. I thought for a moment about the extravagant nature of God's grace and how I could share that with the man outside Union Station. Then I took a twenty-dollar bill, wrapped it around a Billy Graham tract, walked back to Union Station, and dropped it in the man's styrofoam cup. From then on, I always kept a money-wrapped tract in my pocket when I walked the streets of DC. It was the best way I could find not to lose my soul in Washington.

I carried my questions about faith and politics with me to college. Instead of the Naval Academy, I decided to attend a small Christian liberal arts school outside of Philadelphia called Eastern College. Eastern claimed to attempt an integration of faith, reason, and social justice. While I still felt called by God to address the global issues I'd been exposed to in the Third world, I had a thousand questions about what that might mean. Eastern, it seemed, was a place where those questions would be welcome. In my freshman seminar on the classics of Western civilization, I met Phil Cary who taught philosophy and thought carefully about everything. He assigned books and expected us to read them. At the beginning of every class he would look at us with his lively blue eyes, hold the book for that week in his hands, and ask, "What are your questions?" After a year of reading everything from Sophocles to Flannery O'Connor with Dr. Cary, I decided to study philosophy. Teaching me to think with Plato and Aristotle, St. Augustine and St. Thomas Aquinas, Phil Cary helped me to start sorting through the questions I'd brought with me from Washington.

In the middle of this process, the attacks of September 11 happened. I was listening to a lecture on the philosophy of science in the twentieth century when a professor opened the door and informed us that planes had crashed into the World Trade Center and the Pentagon. Class was adjourned. I didn't know what to think. I walked down the hallway to a lobby where students and professors were gathered around a TV screen.

We watched in silence as the scene we would all see hundreds of times unfolded before us. My friend Chris, who was standing beside me, read "American Airlines" on the side of the plane and immediately ran to a pay phone. His dad was a pilot for American and was flying that day.

It was, of course, the personal stories that made September 11 so frightening for everyone. Chris's dad was not on any of the planes that crashed. Over the next few days though, I (like everyone else in America) listened to stories of people who had been affected. And I, like most everyone else, waited to see what our government's response would be. Initial interviews with senators on the street in Washington demonstrated that feelings were mixed. Some cautioned patience. Others demanded immediate retribution. Just what had happened and what our response would be was unclear in the days following September 11.

When *Time* magazine came out later that week, I read Lance Morrow's column entitled "The Case for Rage and Retribution." Morrow was already frustrated by the hesitancy of liberals in Washington. What was needed, he argued, was genuine rage at the horrendous evil that had been done. What he wanted was an immediate act of justice. As I read his words and considered their implications, I felt as if I was looking into a world gone mad.

With the little bit of Christian philosophy that I had under my belt, I wrote a response to Morrow for the October 1 issue of *Time*: "What does it mean to 'toughen up' and give the 'uncivilized' their due," I asked, "when the barbarians are not waiting at the gate but are already among us? To resort to hatred in this crisis is to pull the pin on a hand grenade without having anywhere to throw it." Dr. Cary read my letter in *Time* and engaged me in conversation about just war theory in the Christian tradition. Over the years, he showed me, the church had developed criteria that we should use to consider carefully whether a war is just or not. These just war criteria are based on Paul's assertion in Romans 13 that the State "does not bear the sword in vain." The just war theory says that there are times when it is right to wage war, Dr. Cary told me. There are also, however, times when it is not right. The church has developed criteria over the years to help Christians explain to the State why some wars are unjust.

As Phil Cary was teaching me the careful distinctions that the just war theory helps us to make in times of war, I was also learning about pacifism from the work of the late Mennonite theologian, John Howard Yoder. Yoder recognized Paul's attribution of the "sword" to the State in the book of Romans. God uses governments to restrain evil by means of violence. But Paul is not writing to Christians who run the State in Romans. His readers are people who themselves have been persecuted by the State's sword. Romans 13, then, is not a basis for Christian participation in the State's violence but is, instead, an admonition to suffer patiently the abuse of sinful, broken authorities that God can nevertheless use for his own purposes. I shared this perspective with Dr. Cary. He told me he had a great deal of respect for Mennonites and their commitment to nonviolence as communities of discipleship. He likened it to the pacifism of priests and other religious in the Catholic tradition. Theirs is an important witness, he told me. But it cannot be the church's only position. After all, we live in a world where loving our neighbor sometimes means using force to protect her from an enemy. The U.S. government's war against Afghanistan was a just war, Dr. Cary argued, because it sought to root out the terrorist networks before they could organize to kill other Americans.

Though I respected Dr. Cary, I was not comfortable with his conclusions. As I continued my conversation with him, I was also discussing the same issues with Leah Wilson, my good friend whom I had met on the first day of school at Eastern and to whom I was by that time engaged to be married. Leah was studying sociology at Eastern. The observation Yoder had made about the differing perspectives of first century Christians in the Roman Empire and twenty-first century Christians in America was the sort of thing Leah saw all the time. Her father was a theologian who had studied Yoder carefully and was himself a committed Christian pacifist. While Leah wasn't an absolutist about her own position, she had certainly inherited her father's skepticism about the legitimacy of American foreign policy. Studying sociology at Eastern, she had learned to see the world from the perspective of those who are not in power. Together we spent a lot of time on the streets in Philadelphia, sharing meals with the homeless and learning their perspective on the world, including politics before and after 9/11. They were much less inclined to talk about the justice of

America's wars. Having experienced a great deal of injustice themselves, they didn't stand to gain anything from a war in Afghanistan or anywhere else. They reasoned that a "war on terror" would probably mean that a lot of people they knew would get shipped off with the U.S. Army, only to come home in body bags. A number of these men were Vietnam veterans who'd lost friends and sometimes their own sanity in an unjust war in Southeast Asia. While they didn't have any real alternatives to offer, their critiques were strong and persuasive. They made me want to read more of John Yoder.

After our wedding on December 15, 2001, in King, Leah and I went back to Philadelphia and started attending West Philadelphia Mennonite Fellowship (WPMF). In our new life together we wanted a church community that would encourage us in faithfulness as we tried to follow Jesus. WPMF welcomed us with open arms, inviting us to participate in the worship service during our first month there. In the life of the church, we could see some of the radical alternative that John Yoder wrote about as the "Politics of Jesus." WPMF wasn't perfect, but it certainly gave us hope that there might be a third way between the war making of the American government and the despair of America's critics—both on the streets of Philadelphia and in the "radical left" that was very strong in the West Philadelphia community. The Mennonite church was a school for discipleship in the post-9/11 world. In ways that I couldn't yet understand, our worship there was laying the foundation for the "change of mind" that would mark my conversion to a new understanding of the church's role in the world. I was getting born again.

At the same time that we began worshiping at WPMF, I started a job with the Institute for Global Engagement, a "think-tank with legs" that promotes religious freedom and encourages serious reflection on Christian engagement with global issues. My questions about faith and politics had now turned into a job; I was assigned to write on particularly Christian forms of engagement with the world for the Institute's webzine, *The Brandywine Week in Review* (www.globalengagement.org). As someone who was becoming increasingly more Mennonite, I found myself asking, "What would Yoder say about a 'war on terrorism'?" and "How might the 'politics of Jesus' offer a real alternative in Afghanistan or the Philippines?" I had only been writing for a few months when I began to hear talk about an invasion of Iraq. Could Yoder offer an alternative?

In the spring and summer of 2002 I spent a good deal of time interviewing John Yoder's friends and colleagues about what he might say if he were still alive. In an article titled, "If Yoder Were With Us Now: Theological Reflections on Iraq," I laid out Yoder's conviction that "Jesus is, according to the biblical witness, a model of radical political action." From my interviews, I had begun to imagine a list of practical steps that Yoder might encourage in response to the mounting threat of a war in Iraq. The first was repentance for our own complicity in Saddam's evil and in the devastation of the Iraqi economy and infrastructure—things like admitting that the American government had provided the weapons Saddam used to massacre his own people and that, following the first Gulf War, we had bombed electric facilities, destroyed water-treatment plants, and imposed economic sanctions that prevented hospitals from importing medical supplies. Second, I imagined Yoder calling us to imagine ways we might relieve the suffering we had contributed to. Could we send planes to drop food and medicine before we decided that we had to drop bombs? Perhaps such a reversal of politics as usual would win the goodwill of the Iraqi people. Still, I confessed, Saddam was a problem. Something had to be done about his regime of intimidation and terrorization of the Iraqi people. Yoder's student and friend, Charles Pinches, suggested the questions John might ask: "Who specifically is in trouble? What is the form of their troubles? What can the church do to respond to that specific trouble?" In the end, it seemed, Yoder would insist that those who opposed the violence of Saddam's regime or of the U.S. government against the Iraqi people should be willing to go and suffer with them. Following Jesus, Yoder would insist, means carrying the cross.

In my research I learned that there was an organization called Christian Peacemaker Teams that had begun to mobilize Christians to stand in solidarity with the Iraqi people. Already they were in Baghdad testifying to the widespread effects of economic sanctions and the abuse that some Iraqis had experienced in Saddam's torture cells. I was impressed by their witness and pointed to them in my writing as an example of what it might mean to live out Yoder's vision of the church. Meanwhile, at West Philadelphia Mennonite we were trying to discern what it meant for us to be faithful Christians together as our nation was preparing for war. Just before Christmas, we decided that we would begin the new year with a study of the book of Revelation, paying particular attention to the social context of the Roman Empire in which John wrote his Apocalypse. Our own situation, we felt, was growing increasingly apocalyptic as America began to look more and more like an Empire herself. The Bush administration was using the language of Empire freely, proclaiming *Pax Americana* with all the vigor of a Caesar. Maybe Revelation had something to say to us.

For Christmas, Leah and I visited her parents in California. Discussing politics at dinner one night, someone suggested that we watch the film *Romero*, the story of Archbishop Oscar Romero of El Salvador, who had experienced a conversion to nonviolent peacemaking while serving as bishop during the rule of an oppressive government in his own country. I was deeply struck by two of the movie's scenes. The first was Romero's first sermon in the cathedral at his coronation service as Archbishop. "I come from a world of books," he said slowly, "and there is much to be learned in their pages. But I still have much to learn." Listening, I could feel the tension in myself between the "world of books" and the active life of witness and proclamation that a bishop must live. As a student and a writer, I lived in the world of words. My deep hope was that the pen could be mightier than the sword in this debate about whether America should go to war. But I knew what St. Augustine had said about words—that they are only symbols. Only the ideas that words represent are truly real. For Augustine, to say a word was true was to call it a symbol of something inherent to the very nature of God. Truthful speech alone, though, is not enough in our fallen world. Granted, God spoke things into existence in Genesis. But Jesus taught that the reign of God must be not only proclaimed but also embodied over and against the evil of this world. "The Word became flesh and made his dwelling among us," John's Gospel says. Truth is not merely an idea to be represented with words; truth is a person. Through Christ's body, the church, Augustine had taught me, God calls us beyond our words to engage the world in reality. Romero's words were calling me beyond words to action.

Then his own action did something to me that no movie had ever done. At one point in the movie, the Salvadoran military has occupied the church in Aguilares and is using it as a barracks. Knowing that the occupation is an attempt to intimidate church members who have been speaking out against injustices, Romero goes to the church and says he must remove the sacrament from the altar. The commander of the troops refuses him, shoots the altar with his machine gun, and pushes Romero out the door. After pausing outside, Romero returns, walks past the commander, kneels at the altar, and begins to collect the communion wafers that are now scattered on the floor. Leveling his gun at the altar again, the commander sprays bullets over Romero's head. At their commander's order, soldiers take hold of the Archbishop and carry him out of the church. Romero returns to his car and drives away. But then, as the people of Aguilares watch Romero's car disappear into the dust, the car suddenly turns around and returns. Romero steps out, puts on his robe and stole, and calls the people to come with him to the church and celebrate Mass. The soldiers meet the crowd at the door, their guns in hand. Following their Archbishop, however, the people walk past the guards and reclaim the sanctuary as a place of worship. As I watched the scene I could feel a burning in my stomach that grew hotter as my mind leapt from El Salvador in the late seventies to Iraq in 2002. If the U.S. government insisted on bombing the city of Baghdad, churches and mosques included, someone needed to be there, worshiping God with the Iraqi people. Was God calling me?

I shared my reaction to the movie with Leah in bed that night. She was open to the idea that God might be calling us but said we should probably investigate further what Christian Peacemaker Teams (CPT) was doing in Baghdad. "Surely there are people better qualified than us to go," Leah said. "Would they really want a young couple that hasn't even finished college and is only beginning to become Mennonite?" We agreed that we would contact CPT and let them know that we were willing to go if they needed a couple of folks like us. After all, we thought, plenty of people our age are in the Army Reserves, willing to go to Iraq if the government needs them. Why shouldn't we be willing to go to Iraq if the church needs us?

When we returned to Philadelphia, it was soon my turn in the preaching rotation on the book of Revelation at WPMF. The text I was asked to preach was chapters four and five. To a people suffering the violence of the Roman Empire, John had written about a vision of all the saints in heaven worshiping the Lamb that was slain. The imagery was clear enough: this was Jesus—crucified, yet risen as Lord and King. My question, though, was how such a vision shaped the early church—and how it ought to shape us. At the center of worship in Revelation, I observed, we see the supreme example of God's self-giving love—Jesus as the Lamb that was slain. To be shaped by that vision is to be a people that practices self-giving love. What does it mean to love in the context of war? Doubtless, it means a number of things that it would mean at any time (e.g. performing the traditional works of mercy to our immediate neighbors.) One thing it means specifically in wartime, however, is that some of us ought to be with those who are suffering. The church cannot be silent as nation-states wage war. We must articulate the hope of the kingdom and we must put it into practice. Some of us should be there, I said. But would it be us?

I have to admit that the idea of going frightened me. And not just because I knew that we might not come back alive. I thought about the good people in King who would not understand the conversion that I had experienced over the past few years. Would they feel betrayed, as if I were rejecting them by choosing to stand with the Iraqi people? I couldn't even imagine talking to my parents about the possibility of going—certainly not unless it became a real possibility. They, after all, knew far too well how mixed my motives had been in "following the call" to Africa and Venezuela and Washington and elsewhere. When others had praised me as a "fine young man" who was eager to do God's will, my parents had been able to see that, yes, I did want to follow God. But I wanted a lot of other things too, like adventure and excitement and attention. Would telling them that Leah and I wanted to go to Iraq sound like one more attempt to do something crazy for God? Would they think we were trying to be heroes? Were we? The questions I imagined them asking were, of course, my own questions. They were manifestations of the doubt within my own soul. Leah was much more vocally hesitant than I in our conversations, ready to admit that we were young and inexperienced. Sure, we should be willing to go if God calls us, she said. But we ought not be so arrogant as to think that he wouldn't call a thousand other people before calling us. "But if God does call," I heard those missionary voices saying again, "you have to follow." Would we be able to do it? That question, I think, scared me the most.

We told our parents that going to Iraq was a slight possibility, but shared all our hesitations. "It probably won't happen," we assured them. "We just wanted you to know what we're thinking." In February Leah and I packed our bags and carried all those questions with us to visit my friend Marty in El Salvador. He had been there for nearly a year, working with Samaritan's Purse (SP) on a disaster relief project. After a few days of showing us the houses and animal projects that SP had undertaken in a number of villages throughout the Salvadoran countryside, Marty took a day off work and gave us a tour of the capital city, San Salvador, beginning at the cathedral where Romero had served as Archbishop. We visited Romero's tomb and read the words of the Salvadoran people on cards and banners that filled the crypt. The man whose story had so inspired me was clearly an inspiration to his own country. To the people of El Salvador, Oscar Romero was a saint.

It was in the afternoon, after we had visited Romero's tomb, that I checked my e-mail at Marty's office and read a short message from the CPT office in Chicago asking if Leah and I could leave on March 18 for Baghdad. All the questions we had brought with us were suddenly reduced to one: yes or no? Romero was on our mind, reminding us of the truth of the cross. Sometimes God calls Christians to die for the sake of the kingdom. We were not, however, eager to become martyrs. Leah and I had only been married for fourteen months and had all the dreams of a long, happy life together that most young couples hope for. We were scheduled to graduate from Eastern in May, but walking away from our last semester of classes meant that there was no guarantee that we could do so. There were plenty of good reasons, we thought, to say no. Yet, we had said that if God called, we were willing to follow. More specifically, we had promised God that if CPT needed us to go to Baghdad, we would go. It was good for us to be able to talk with Marty. He loved us as much as any human being can, but was not pulled by the protective instinct that would color our conversations with our parents. He listened as we processed out loud, repeating conversations that we had been having now for two months. Finally, we said we had to go.

Talking with our parents was not easy. They were resistant, asking all the questions we had been asking ourselves, but sometimes making us feel like they didn't think we'd been mature enough to ask them already. It wasn't fun. We had to admit that we hadn't been as transparent as we could have been about the process we'd gone through in deciding to go. We had not, for example, shared our thoughts with Leah's parents when we began thinking about the possibility of joining CPT while visiting them over Christmas. I don't know that I had really explained to my parents why we became Mennonite. How could we expect them to understand? Yet, in a sense, they did. When we talked about what we heard God saying, I could sense that they trusted us. They never suspected us of using God's call as a cover for our own designs. (Something I had suspected myself of doing more than once in my own life.) The Jesus we were wrestling with was the Jesus they had taught us to follow as children. Their faith was strong enough that they could believe God would not lead us astray.

Still, they knew faith was something that had to be examined. When we explained the situation with the peace team in Iraq, my dad understood that we would be breaking U.S. sanctions by traveling there and could be subject to fines or imprisonment. "Doesn't God call us to obey the law of the land?" he asked. It was a good question. As my parents shared our decision with friends in King, they called back with more questions: Did we think there was an alternative way to get rid of Saddam? Didn't the threat of nuclear weapons that could destroy millions of lives merit some sort of preemptive action? Were we questioning President Bush's ability to hear the call of God? And what about people in our church who had served in the armed forces? Did we not think they were Christians?

It was with all these questions in mind that Leah and I sat down to write a letter to our family, friends, and churches, explaining our decision to go to Iraq. We decided to make three simple points: first of all, the church had called us. Like all those soldiers who were willing to risk their lives because of the call of our government, we were willing to take a risk at the call of the church. Secondly, we noted that there were more than seven hundred thousand Christians in Iraq. Not only had the church called us, but we were going to be with the church—a persecuted church that had been hard pressed for some time by our government's policies and was now facing the prospect of being bombed and occupied by U.S. forces. Finally, we said, we were thinking about the future of Christian missions in the Middle East. While we weren't going to proselytize Iraqis in a time of war, we did believe that Muslims in the Middle East should have the opportunity to hear the good news of Jesus Christ. Unfortunately, we knew, the Arab world was becoming increasingly closed to Christian missions because of their identification of Christianity with a militant West. If some Christians are not there with the Iraqi people as they are being bombed, we said, then they will never want to hear that Jesus loves them.

At the heart of our decision, we tried to make clear, was a deep desire to be the salt of the earth at a time when the world sorely needed it. Behind that desire was a long series of conversions that I could not explain to anyone in a single conversation. As we began to talk about our decision, though, I was increasingly confident that it was God's voice we had heard calling us. It was, indeed, years of following Jesus that had brought me to this place. "When Jesus calls a man," Dietrich Bonhoeffer wrote in *The Cost of Discipleship*, "he bids him come and die." Getting baptized at the age of seven had been my initiation into this way of dying. When Preacher Yates dunked me in that baptismal pool, he killed me. But God raised me from the dead into a life where death is never the last word. To carry a cross is to know that our peculiarly Christian way of living is marked by a willingness to die in order to live. The God who raised Jesus from the dead gives us the hope we need to "face death daily," as Paul said. "When Jesus calls a man, he bids him come and die"—and, in dying, to find the life that is truly life.

As we prepared to leave for Iraq, the question of whether we were ready to die was the one that people who loved us kept asking. In the midst of all our last minute preparations, I met with our pastor, Fred, at WPMF. "How is your family responding?" he asked. "They're very supportive," I said. "But they don't want to see us die." Fred smiled. "We want to see you come back in one piece as well," he affirmed. "But I'm quite certain that, in a very real sense, you will die."

Fred was right. Facing my country's guns and praying to dodge its bombs, I died in Iraq. No longer could I be thankful for the comfort and security that bombs provided (whether directly or indirectly) after meeting children maimed by shrapnel. No longer could I enjoy the blessings of economic prosperity after meeting people whose lives have been destroyed by U.S.-driven economic policy. No longer could I believe in the violent use of power to liberate a people after hearing them say, "If this is democracy, we don't want it; if this is liberation, you can keep it." But no longer could I bear to listen to the liberals either. No longer could I say, "Let's wait just a little while longer," after meeting the Iraqi people who had lived in fear of Saddam for so long. No longer could I say, "Diplomacy is the answer," after seeing how the United Nations had utterly failed in its attempts to help the Iraqi people. No longer could I say, "Peace, peace," where there was no peace. All of my options crumbled in the horrible face of sin-wrecked humanity in Iraq.

When God called us to Baghdad, we followed to a death. My worldview was crushed into a thousand pieces and scattered to the wind. In a public forum with the other students and faculty at Eastern the night before we left for the Middle East, I explained the just war theory that Dr. Cary had taught me to use so carefully. Dr. Cary and I had agreed in conversation that the proposed preemptive invasion of Iraq could not be justified by anyone who took the classic just war theory seriously. I challenged anyone in the room that night to stand up and explain how a war against Iraq could be just. Silence. Yet, in a vote the next day, the student body rejected a statement opposing the war. Eastern's community was a microcosm of the American church. Despite clear condemnation of the proposed war by Pope John Paul II, Archbishop of Canterbury Rowan Williams, and almost every major denomination in the United States, tens of thousands of committed church members were already stationed in the Gulf, poised to fight. The just war theory, it seemed, simply wasn't working.

Beyond the tools that I had learned to use in studying the Christian tradition, I had also learned the classic distinction between liberals and conservatives in American politics. I had grown up conservative, my parents being registered Republicans. My growing concern for social justice issues had opened my eyes to concerns that would be considered liberal—things like health care, racial justice, and the environment. Still, I didn't consider myself a Democrat. As my worldview crumbled in the face of Iraq, I began to doubt seriously that the classic conservative/liberal option was really an option at all. Both parties seemed to bow to the madness of war. None of the choices on the table seemed legitimate. The tools that America had given me also failed.

Twenty-four hours after President Bush had announced his forty-eight-hour ultimatum for Saddam Hussein and his sons to leave Iraq, Leah and I boarded an overnight flight from New York's JFK airport to Amman, Jordan. CPT had not known that the timing would be so close when they'd begun planning the trip some months earlier. Nor had we when we decided to go. But as we stumbled forward in our attempt to follow God's call, I was hopeful. The darkness into which we were flying promised a third way that I could not yet see, as all of my intellectual dichotomies crumbled. The approaching death that was now inevitable promised new life, though I didn't have the slightest clue what it would look like. In the seat in front of us were Jerry and Sis Levin, also members of the CPT delegation. As we boarded the plane they told us they had made this trip before. I didn't know, as I fell asleep that night, how important they would be in showing us the way.

II.

A COMMUNION OF SAINTS

We met Jerry and Sis Levin in the Royal Jordanian waiting area at JFK International Airport. Our flight for Jordan was leaving late in the evening, and it had been a long day for all of us. I was talking on a pay phone to my parents, filling them in on some details before leaving the country, when Jerry realized we were with the CPT delegation and extended a very energetic greeting. Though I didn't know it at the time, this was Jerry's standard greeting. He was talking and waving his hands before he ever got to me. I had to break off my phone conversation to introduce myself. I don't think Jerry even realized I was on the phone. He took me over to meet Sis, who was all smiles, even as she propped up an injured ankle on her suitcase. "I fell off a cliff in the Galilee," she offered in a lilting Southern accent that reminded me of *Gone With the Wind*. What Sis didn't explain then was why a grandmother in her early seventies was hiking around the Galilee.

Jerry and Sis told us their story over dinner a couple of nights later in Amman. It was Jerry's birthday and they were reminiscing about their first trip to the Middle East some twenty years earlier. Jerry, who worked for CNN at the time, had been sent to Beirut to serve as their Middle East Bureau Chief. That was in 1983. Shortly after their arrival, U.S. peacekeeping forces had pulled out of Lebanon on the *U.S.S.*

New Jersey, firing at the hillsides above Beirut as they left. The Lebanese were not pleased, and the more militant among them became hostile toward Americans. It wasn't very long afterward that Jerry was taken hostage while on his way to work one morning. His captors were an Islamic terrorist organization named Hezbollah.

In her book, *Beirut Diaries*, Sis tells the story of her education in Middle East politics as she worked for nearly a year to negotiate Jerry's release. Initially, the CIA told her to stay quiet and let them handle the situation. Not knowing any better, Sis decided to do as she was told. After a few months, though, she began to realize that the CIA had no interest in getting Jerry out. So Sis decided to get him out herself (with a good deal of help from an impressive host of characters). The book is a fascinating read and quite an education in itself. Sis and Jerry were giving us the highlights during our dinner conversation.

I was struck by Sis's own astonishment at how politics in the Middle East really works. Though her initial naïveté may have been a bit exaggerated for dramatic effect in her telling of the story, Sis had seen something about her own government that had astounded her as an American citizen. Eager to find her husband and get him back, Sis had talked with and listened to nearly every person of influence in the Arab world. As she listened, she had begun to hear stories of bitterness about the United States and its history in the Middle East. Though Jerry certainly didn't deserve to have been taken hostage, it became clear to her that no American's hands were clean in this situation. She was most touched by a story she heard from one of Jerry's fellow captives, Marty Jenko, after he was released.

Blindfolded, shackled, and held in solitary confinement, Marty had almost no human contact during his captivity. The only people he could possibly connect with were his guards. Over time, Marty developed a friendship with a guard named Hajh. At night, Hajh would sometimes take Marty onto the roof and let him lie on his back and look at the stars. One night, as they lay next to each other on the roof, Hajh whispered to Marty, "Will you forgive me?" After a pause Marty replied, "Will you forgive me?" Marty, like Sis, had come to realize his own complicity in the violence of the Middle East.

What Sis hadn't known as her eyes were being opened to the realities of American/Middle East relations was how Jerry's time in solitary confinement was opening his eyes in other ways. As we ate pita and hummus that night in Amman, Jerry told us how he had begun to ask questions about his captors and their political situation and, finally, about the God who had created both him and them. Fifty years old at the time, Jerry had considered himself an atheist for most of his life. All alone in the darkness behind his blindfold, he said he needed someone to talk to. "I couldn't talk to someone who wasn't real," Jerry explained. "I had to believe in God."

For Christmas Jerry's captors had offered to bring him a gift. He asked for a Bible. Already committed to the God of its pages, Jerry pored over Jesus' words about loving enemies and blessing those who persecute you. In a damp, cold cell, he heard a call to practice the peacemaking of Jesus in the Middle East. He smiled his awkward grin. "So that's what we've been doing ever since."

In typical style, Jerry offered us this one-liner: "So a secular Jew gets taken hostage by some militant Muslims and becomes an evangelical Christian. Go figure." With her deceptively innocent-sounding voice, Sis added, as if it were the most normal thing in the world, "Now we're working to reconcile the dysfunctional family of Abraham." Both Jerry and Sis thanked God that evening for all he had done to bring them to that place. "I'm grateful to the Hezbollah," Jerry said, "for giving me a year of solitude. In all my years of chasing the next news story, I'd never really stopped to think about the things that really matter." When he and Sis were forced to stop, they had been transformed into laborers for God's kingdom and peace.

Leah and I enjoy telling people that we were the youngest and most inexperienced members of our delegation to Iraq. Our average age was sixty, the predominant hair color gray. (That is, for those who still had hair.) Like Jerry and Sis, though, all the people we met had stories to tell about how God had changed their lives and given them a vision for his kingdom. Leah and I had worried before leaving home about our own inexperience in peacemaking and our confusion about politics. As we met our fellow teammates, our worries subsided to a sense of amazement. I think it fair to say that we lived off the spiritual capital of our fellow peacemakers while in the Middle East.

No one impressed us more than Jim Douglass. We were told that Jim would meet us in Amman because he was coming from Rome. When we finally arrived at the Al Monzer, our little hotel just off the bus circle, Jamil at the desk phoned Jim in his room to tell him we had arrived. When Jim came down he greeted Jerry and Sis warmly. I could tell they were friends. Then Jerry turned to introduce Jim to us. "Wonderful to meet you," Jim said as he smiled and squinted his eyes behind horn-rimmed glasses. He extended his arms to hug us as if we had been friends for years. Leah says she could tell from the minute she met Jim that he was a saint.

Jerry was anxious to hear from Jim how his trip to Rome had gone. As we would later learn, Jim had a number of connections with cardinals at the Vatican, whom he had befriended during his work for conscientious objection and against nuclear war during the Vatican II Council in the mid-sixties. Before going to Rome, Jim had traveled to New York to visit the Iraqi embassy at the United Nations. "If I can persuade the Pope to go to Baghdad," Jim had asked, "would you grant him a visa?" The Iraqi officials in New York had communicated with Baghdad and assured Jim that, if the Pope was willing to go, he would be welcome in Iraq. Jim's next step, then, was to travel to Rome and try to convince the Pope to go with him to Amman. His plan was to fast and pray in St. Peter's Square and request meetings with the cardinals he knew. The cardinals came out to meet with Jim, thanking him for his witness and encouraging him that the Pope was very much in support of his trip. Each time Jim asked to speak to the Pope, however, he hit a brick wall. "The Pope is too frail to travel," one cardinal said. "But he's planning a trip to Spain next month," Jim replied. Despite his persistence, the Cardinals didn't budge. "The Pope, I'm afraid, has his own human shields," Jim told us with a mischievous smile. "They knew if I'd asked him he would have wanted to go."

At lunch the next day, Leah and I got a chance to talk with Jim. By that time, we were well aware that we had much to learn from his experience. "So how did you get into this?" I asked him. "I think it was Dorothy Day," Jim said. "She looked at me one day and said, 'Jim, you're a wonder.' And she was right, of course, because we're all wonders. She could see that." When Jim was a freshman in college, his English professor, Herbert Burke, had given the class an article about Dorothy Day and her "Catholic Workers" refusing to go underground in New York City during a nuclear fallout drill. Professor Burke asked the class to respond. Jim was offended by the story and didn't understand why Catholics would break the law and get arrested. The more he argued his point, however, the more he learned about the threat of nuclear war and the position of those who refused to obey a law that assumed nuclear war was inevitable. The bomb, Jim came to believe, was America's ultimate symbol of our failure to trust God.

Day and the *Catholic Worker* newspaper became important teachers for Jim. There he learned about the Catholic Church's social teachings and the work of those who sought to live an alternative to the violence of this world in houses of hospitality. Jim was captivated by Jesus' call to peacemaking and made it the focus of his graduate studies. His work in Rome during Vatican II was an attempt to apply what he had learned to the official policy of the Roman Catholic Church. The church must make clear, he argued, that those who feel they should not fight in war for reasons of conscience ought not to fight. And nuclear war must be condemned, Jim insisted. In the end, the Council agreed.

After Vatican II, Jim taught theology for a number of years, moving from one college to the next as his commitment to active nonviolence inevitably made the administration of the school uncomfortable. It was while teaching at the University of Honolulu that Jim, his wife Shelly, and others in a group called Catholic Action began distributing leaflets outside Hickam Air Force Base. Through their investigation of the war in Vietnam, Catholic Action of Hawaii had learned that Hickam was the center for "electronic warfare" in Southeast Asia. In the jungles of Vietnam, Cambodia, and Laos, the U.S. government had placed electronic sensors to detect any motion. The sensors could not distinguish between a troop of guerilla fighters, a wild animal, and a child playing in the jungle. Wherever there was movement, the sensors triggered a computer at Hickam Air Force Base, and a missile was launched into the jungle. The U.S. government had made a calculated decision to shoot anything that moves. Jim and the

Catholic Action group wanted the men and women who worked at Hickam to know what they were doing. They stood outside the gates of the base on one day a week and handed out leaflets that explained the details of electronic warfare and their own evaluation of its ethical implications.

One morning as Jim was driving to the base, he got in the wrong lane of traffic and ended up driving through the gates. Inside, he thought he would look around and see what he could learn. To his amazement, no one stopped him as he drove to the main building, parked his car, and walked inside. On a directory in the lobby, he saw the listing for "Director of Electronic Warfare." Curious to see how close he could get, Jim walked all the way to the office, stopping once to ask a soldier for directions. Then he turned around, went back to his car, and drove home. He had an idea.

The next week Jim and a couple of friends returned to the base, following the same course Jim had inadvertently discovered the week before. In a briefcase Jim was carrying a letter to the Director of Electronic Warfare, explaining his objections to the practices of the U.S. military. He also had a plastic bottle filled with his own blood. Jim returned to the office he had found the week before, knocked on the door, and was greeted by a young soldier who introduced himself as the secretary to the Director of Electronic Warfare. Jim said that he had a letter to deliver to the Director. The soldier said he would take it into the Director's office right away, leaving Jim alone in the room. Behind the secretary's desk, Jim saw a file cabinet marked "Top Secret" with its top drawer standing open. He stepped around the desk, opened his bottle, and began pouring blood onto the files. The next thing Jim knew, he was on the floor with a soldier's knee in his back. "Don't give me any of your philosophy," Jim heard the soldier say.

Jim's symbolic act of resistance to the violence of electronic warfare landed him in a Honolulu courtroom, where he had to defend himself for his actions. But he did not feel that they were entirely defensible. By that time Jim realized his own violence in the action. Choosing to break the law was not something he was opposed to in principle, but he had agreed with Shelley that he would not at that particular time. (For a number of reasons, they had decided that it made more sense for Shelley to get arrested, not Jim.) He had broken her trust. Attempting to resist the violence of war, Jim knew that he was guilty of doing violence to Shelley. His hands were not clean. But the government's certainly were not either. Jim realized that the prosecution was caught in a dilemma. If they brought the files into court, he could demonstrate that the U.S. government was in violation of international law. If they refused, there was no evidence against him. With that, the case was over. (The judge actually resigned from the case, forcing a second judge to charge Jim with a misdemeanor.) Jim walked away with a small fine that he refused to pay. His contract at the University of Honolulu, however, was not renewed. He and Shelley returned to Hedley, British Columbia, Jim's hometown.

Thousands of miles from the courtroom in Honolulu, Jim and Shelley were surprised one day by a visit from Bob Aldridge, a man who had heard about Jim's action and had gone to Honolulu with his wife, Janet, to witness the trial. Bob had been an engineer for Lockheed who worked for years on a Pentagon project to develop Trident missiles that could serve as "first strike" weapons from the sea in a nuclear war. Learning about Jim's resistance in the midst of a struggle within his own conscience (a struggle that his daughter's questions about her father's work had sparked), Bob had quit his job and come to ask Jim what he should do. So began the "Trident Campaign" to stop the submarines Bob had designed to win the Cold War by making the "first strike" in a battle that could literally destroy the world. Jim and Shelley had devoted much of their life to persuading those who worked on the submarines and their government overseers that nuclear war was not the answer. Jesus offered us another way forward. That way of Jesus was something Jim believed in because he had experienced it in his own life. His personal faith, it seemed, had given him a viable political alternative to all the available options. Listening to Jim, I got excited. Was this the "third way" I had been searching for?

CPT had planned for our delegation to fly into Amman, stay the night at Al Monzer, get our visas from the Iraqi embassy, and leave early the next morning for Baghdad. But the night we arrived in Amman, Bush's forty-eight-hour ultimatum was up. Would the bombs start falling in the night? If they did, was there any hope of making it

31

to Baghdad? Leah and I went to our room exhausted. We had had very little sleep for days as we made last minute preparations to leave home, and we had taken an overnight flight to Jordan. As we lay in bed, wondering what we might wake up to in the morning, the wind of a dust storm beat against our window. Then, for the first time, I heard the call to prayer from a minaret just across the street. All of the Muslim world, I knew, was praying tonight for the people of Iraq. I, too, should pray. I got out of bed, switched on a small light, and wrote my prayer as a poem.

Restless on the brink of war
Waged in the name of liberty,
I hear a caller cry to the Merciful
In words I cannot understand.
Wild winds howl outside my window
And on across the desert to Iraq,
Blowing dust into faces determined
To bring freedom by the power of the sword.

How long, we ask, until the bombs fall?
How long until this ugly war is done?
The cries in Arabic, caught up by wind,
Ask the psalmist's question again:
"How long, O Lord, will you forget us forever?"
With the saints around God's throne, we moan
In anguish without words to speak
The sorrow that eclipses sleep.

And yet beyond the sun, behind the wind,
Upon the throne we strive to see
There sits a Lamb in whom we trust,
Our God and Lord and King.
The victory we wait for
Is the war that he has won,
Giving himself on the cross
To defeat the evil one.

And every knee shall bend and bow
When he comes again as Lord.
Where is this King of glory now?
How long until his coming?
I hear him in the wild wind.
I see him in the suffering child.
And I know that he is listening
To prayers I cannot understand.

Sometime after midnight I fell asleep. When I woke, it was still dark outside. I walked down to the lobby, where a couple of guests from this small hotel were gathered around the television. The Arabic news station, one of them told me in English, had announced that the war had begun. They switched to CNN and we watched footage of a missile being launched. Saddam, the anchor said, was the missile's target. "Saddam is not in the palace," one man shouted back at the television. "Saddam is in a taxi in the streets. He's in the people's houses." He slumped back into the couch, covered his face with his hands, and began to weep. Salim, I later learned, was the man's name. Baghdad was his hometown. And he was a Christian. During the first night of Operation Iraqi Freedom, Salim and I cried together in the lobby of the Al Monzer hotel.

Our delegation of nine met early that next morning for an update on the night's events and a time of worship together. Together we prayed a simple litany, repeating a refrain: "The Lord of cosmic power, Jacob's God will shield us." CPT had been clear in saying to the media that we were not traveling to Iraq as human shields, Westerners whom Saddam had courted to come and stay in places of his choosing so that the U.S. government might not bomb there. We were not human shields; instead, God was our shield. Jim suggested that the communion of saints might be part of God's shield for us, and wondered out loud whether some of his own friends who had died, like Phil Berrigan and Thomas Merton, might not be watching over us as we prepared to go into a war zone. Calling our attention to the living dead—the communion of saints—Jim was reminding us, I think, of the strange logic of the cross. That God would shield us did not necessarily mean we would not be harmed. It meant we could carry on in the hope of resurrection. At this point all of our delegation's plans were falling apart. Hope was the only way forward.

Without a letter from the Foreign Ministry in Baghdad approving our visas, we could not enter Iraq. The letter had not yet come. And the Foreign Ministry office, CNN reported, had been bombed during the night. We sent someone to wait in line at the embassy and ask if the letter had come. The answer was, "No, you can come back tomorrow." It was a response we got used to over the next few days.

Our strategy was to send a different person down to the embassy after each rejection to ask again. Meanwhile, the rest of the team waited, prayed, listened to reports on the situation in Baghdad, and considered whether we should perhaps abort our plans to go to Baghdad and join the CPT team in Hebron, West Bank. We met with representatives of relief organizations that planned to go into Iraq as soon as the invasion was completed and with the American Friends Service Committee that was monitoring the situation closely. The more people we talked to, the less likely it seemed that we would be able to make it to Baghdad. Even if the visas came through, which was unlikely, those who knew the road from Jordan to Baghdad cautioned us against taking it. One man told us about a reporter who had nearly died on that road during the first Gulf War when the car he was riding in was hit by a missile from a fighter jet. He and his driver had jumped from the car just seconds before they watched it explode in flames. The U.S. position at that time had been to shoot anything that moved on the road. This time, our consultant suspected, the planes flying overhead would patrol the highway in much the same way.

Watching and waiting, we felt helpless. Sure, we could pray. But couldn't we have done that from our homes in the States? Sister Anne Montgomery, a seasoned peace activist, had come over from the West Bank to join our delegation. As we waited, she shared with us one morning how she was struggling with depression, eager to be with fellow Sisters at a convent in Iraq whom she knew well and was worried about, but unable to do anything. "I feel helpless," she said. "But I realize my solidarity with the Iraqi people as I pray to God in desperation." We, like they, were helpless.

I had tea with a Jordanian businessman, Jamil, who shared with me his perspective on the helplessness of the Iraqi (and Palestinian) people. "You have to realize," he said to me, "they cannot dream. These people feel like screws in a machine." It was a powerful image to consider as I listened to reporters on CNN talk about the "surgical precision" of the war machine that was destroying real people's lives. Screws in a machine have no dignity, of course. They are replaceable parts. To be used and abused, in American slang, is to get screwed over. Jamil helped me begin to understand the desperation that produces suicide bombers. When a machine goes crazy, running out of order, the best thing a screw can do is snap, stopping the machine. When that's the only viable option in one's power, it makes sense to do it. It makes sense in the same way that bombing Iraq made sense to the United States because it was all that we could do in a desperate situation. Might our solidarity in desperation with both the Iraqi people and the U.S. government, however, push us toward an alternative? "We must find a third way," I scribbled in my journal. "Neither the violence of the powerful (war) nor the violence of the weak (terrorism). What we must accept is the violence of love—the violence we take upon ourselves for the sake of Jesus and his kingdom. 'Whosoever would be my disciple must take up his cross and follow me.'"

As we waited, Jerry suggested we have a "teach-in," taking advantage of the incredible resources that existed within our little community that was beginning to take shape. Jim Douglass, Jerry reminded us, was an authority on the theology of nonviolence. Would he give us an introductory course? Jim agreed. He began by presenting us with the problem that had most troubled him in his sixty-five years of learning to follow Jesus. "The troubling thing for me has been that I believe Jesus' greatest disciple in the twentieth century was a Hindu." Jim was referring to Gandhi. The only Gandhi I really knew as I listened to Jim was a good man who, nevertheless, didn't know Jesus. Growing up in evangelical churches, I had heard more than one sermon in which Gandhi was held up as the prime example of one who simply didn't understand the doctrine of justification by faith. He thought he could work his way to heaven, my pastors had said. But he was wrong.

Even still, I had heard at least one sermon in which Gandhi was held up as a challenge to the church. "I like your Christ, but I don't like your Christians," Gandhi had said. Did the challenge of this "little brown man," as the preacher described him, call us to be better Christians? Jim thought so. As a Catholic, Jim had read carefully the stories of Gandhi's engagement with Christianity, the religion of his British oppressors in India. Jim told us that on Gandhi's visit to the Vatican, a crucifix had brought him to tears. "Living Christ is a living cross," Gandhi had said to some of his Christian friends. "Without it life is a living death." The cross, Gandhi had seen, was the symbol of a way in which Jesus called people to live their lives. Though he stubbornly refused some of the doctrines of Christianity (what good were they anyway if they really didn't make any difference in Christians' lives?), Gandhi had committed himself to this way of the cross more radically perhaps than anyone else in the twentieth century. "Without wealth, position, or authority," Jim said, "Gandhi became the most powerful person in India." By the grace of God, he had stumbled upon the politics of the cross.

Challenged by Gandhi, Jim had been forced again in his theological studies to ask the question, "Who was Jesus?" Jesus himself said that he was the "Son of Man," a somewhat enigmatic phrase that is a literal translation of an Aramaic idiom which means "the human being." Jesus, then, seemed to suggest in his own self-naming that he was *the* example of what it means to live as God meant for humans to live. The church confesses that Jesus is fully God and fully human. In him, we see God's new humanity, the new creation that is, and is coming, in the kingdom of God.

Jesus' proclamation of the kingdom of God occurred in a political context. Two cities, Sepphoris and Jerusalem, represented the political alternatives in Jesus' day. In Sepphoris, Jim said, just miles from Jesus' hometown of Nazareth, some Zealots had led a violent uprising during Jesus' youth that resulted in the destruction of the entire city. The terrorism of the Zealots, then, stood as one political option that had been tried and found wanting. On the other hand, there was the city of Jerusalem, the political center of Israel. There the religious leaders of Jesus' day had learned to cooperate with the Romans, joining with them in the violent oppression of the masses that often resulted in public crucifixions as a reminder of Rome's power. On the one hand was the Zealot option; on the other, accommodation with the power of Empire. Jesus, Jim said, rejected both. Proclaiming the advent of the kingdom of God, Jesus invited his followers to learn the life of a new humanity and so become the beloved community of God. Central to this new politics was a commitment to the cross. Jesus would refuse both the violence of the powerful and the violence of the weak. Instead, he would suffer the violence of crucifixion, giving himself for the sake of those who hated him. Jesus insisted that there was power in the cross. "Do not return evil for evil," Paul said, summarizing Jesus, "but overcome evil with good." Gandhi had shown us that the politics of Jesus is really possible, Jim said. But only God could give us the strength to do it.

As Jim concluded, my mind was racing. Telling the story of his own attempt to follow Jesus, he had given me the language I so needed to articulate the third way of Jesus as a real, practicable alternative. The key to the new political vision I was looking for was Jesus' reinterpretation of *the* city—the *polis*, to make the root word connection—Jerusalem. In the world of ancient Israel, Jerusalem was the center of Jewish life, and at its center was the temple. The temple served both symbolically and functionally as the center of economic, political, and religious life in Israel. It was Wall Street, Washington, and Vatican City all wrapped up in one. Symbolically, there was nothing more important to Jesus' contemporaries than their holy city, Jerusalem, and its temple. This is why the city/temple language Jesus used was so important. "You are the light of the world," Jesus had said to his rag-tag band of followers who were gathered on a hillside outside the city. "A city set on a hill cannot be hidden." Where was this Jerusalem? Jerusalem is here, Jesus said to those who would follow him. Jerusalem is now because Jerusalem is us.

That Israel had been defiled by occupation forces from Rome was a fact that every Jew had learned to accept in Jesus' day. What the people of Israel clung to, however, was their Holy City and its temple. No one was going to take it from them. The Jewish historian Josephus tells of a time when troops were sent by Pontius Pilate to carry Roman standards, symbols of the imperial authority, into Jerusalem. A popular movement of thousands met the troops on their way to the temple, laid down in front of them, and requested that the troops kill them before defiling the temple.

The passion of that scene before the temple mount sheds light on the emotion that Jesus' cleansing of the temple must have provoked. Turning over tables and casting out the money-changers, Jesus demonstrated his condemnation of the exploitation that was taking place in his Father's house. "Tear this temple down," Jesus said, "and I will rebuild it in three days." In light of his resurrection, the message becomes clear: "*I* am the temple," Jesus is saying. "My *body* is the dwelling place of God." A new political institution is established in Jesus' resurrected body.

But still the question: Where is this temple? Where is the New Jerusalem where we can see this new way of living together? Paul discovered the answer for the early church while on the road to Damascus. An official of the old temple at the time, Paul's mission was to round up the Christians in Damascus and bring them bound to Jerusalem. On his way there, however, he was blinded by a "bright light from heaven" and heard the voice of Jesus himself.

"Why are you persecuting me?" the risen Jesus asked. Paul was confused. What did Jesus' question mean? Paul was on his way to arrest the followers of Jesus, not Jesus himself. After all, Jesus has been dead for some time now. The voice, however, was clear: "Why are you persecuting *me*?" To persecute Jesus' people, the church, was to persecute the living Christ. In some ineffable way, Paul saw, the rabbi and his disciples had become one.

Out of this experience Paul went on to develop his understanding of the church as Christ's body. Having learned the story of Jesus' Last Supper with his disciples, Paul realized that, "Take, eat; this is my body," was an invitation to be members of the mysterious community that lives and acts as Jesus' body, the new temple for all nations. "For in one Spirit we are all baptized into one body," Paul wrote to the church at Corinth. Wherever we gather in that one Spirit, the temple is there. Jerusalem is there. The beloved community is now the center of our economic, political, and religious life. Sharing our possessions, we leave no one in need. Pledging our allegiance to God, we refuse to serve nationalistic idols. Worshipping our risen Savior, we receive his forgiveness for our sins. We who exist as the body of Christ are the New Jerusalem now.

The politics of Jesus, I was beginning to see, do not set forth an ideal that we hope for in the next world, while resigning ourselves to choose between more realistic options in this world. Instead, they teach us what it means to live as the church in our world. Furthermore, they offer the only plausible hope for the future of humanity. When Jesus offered himself as a sacrifice for us, he presented humanity with a way out of the inevitable destruction that is the result of sin. Because of God's great love, the option is always before us. We are invited to live out God's way in this world until the kingdoms of this world become the kingdom of our God.

As this new political vision of the church was coming together in my head, I looked around the room and realized I was sitting in the midst of the new community that Jesus had made possible. Praying for the Spirit to guide us, we were experiencing the truth of Jesus' new humanity. As we waited, there was time to get to know one another. I could see that God's great gift to me on this journey was a communion of saints who were eager to follow his call. What Jesus had said was true: "No one who leaves father and mother and sister and brother for my sake will fail to receive a hundred times as much in this present age." Having offered ourselves to God, we found that God had opened his family to us.

God's instruments of grace were certainly not limited to those of us who were part of the CPT delegation. Jamil, a young man who worked at the desk in Al Monzer, became a good friend to a number of us as we waited to see whether the door to Baghdad would open. "I think you will be able to go," he said to me. I told Jamil that if we did go, I was a little worried about how the Iraqis would receive us. "I don't speak Arabic," I told him, "but I want the people we meet to understand that we've come to be with them in this very difficult time because we love them. We're sorry that our country has decided to bomb them. We want to try to live another way together with them…."

"Don't worry," Jamil interrupted. He shook his finger back and forth in front of my face. "If you are there when bombs are falling, they will understand." Jamil slapped me on the back and laughed. I felt that he was right about the Iraqi people. But was he right about us making it to Baghdad? Everyone who went down to the Embassy was still getting the same response. "No, the letter has not come. Please come back tomorrow." Though the delegation felt strongly that we had been called to go to Iraq, we could not justify sitting in Amman any longer. We decided to give it one last try at the Embassy. If it didn't work, we were going to join the CPT team in the West Bank.

Kara, the Catholic laywoman we had sent to make the last attempt, came into our meeting room with a smile on her face. "I got a visa!" she said, holding the paper up for us to see. "But I only got one." An official at the Embassy had agreed to give Kara a visa for herself, but said he could not grant visas for the whole delegation. We decided to send Dave, an Anglican deacon from England, back with Kara to say that he did not want her to travel to Baghdad alone. He put his collar on as he headed out the door. "Maybe this will help." The Iraqi official was persuaded by Dave's case and agreed to grant him a visa. But he made it clear that he could give no more. Dave and Kara could go to Baghdad, but the rest of the delegation would have to stay behind.

After some discussion and prayer, we decided that God had called us to Iraq as a delegation and, if he wanted us to be there, he could make a way. The God we serve, after all, was just as much Lord of the Iraqi Embassy as he was of our lives. Whether the officials knew it or not, God could use them. Maybe we just needed to take one more step. All nine of us decided to hail taxis and return to the Embassy together. The official with whom Kara and Dave had worked was not happy to see us. He repeated to them that he could not grant any more visas. His frustration at our repeated request was visible. We would have to leave, he said. There was nothing he could do.

But the next morning, we came back. All of us together, lined up in the waiting room, watched as Jerry went to the window. "Can we get visas today?" he asked. "No, the letter has not come," the man on the other side of the window responded. "Please come back tomorrow." "But the letter isn't going to come," Jerry exclaimed. "Isn't there anything else we can do to get visas?" "Have you spoken to Mr. Jamal?" the man asked. Mr. Jamal? Who was he? "No, we haven't," Jerry said. "Can we?" The official scribbled a phone number on a piece of paper and handed it to Jerry who walked outside, found a payphone, and called immediately. Mr. Jamal said he would meet with us.

Entering the Embassy through another door, we were welcomed into a much nicer waiting area and told that Mr. Jamal would be with us shortly. Five minutes later, a short, balding Iraqi man in a very nice business suit greeted us and asked why we wanted to go to Baghdad. We were quick to give him reasons: we wanted to be with the Iraqi people; we wanted to be a witness for peace; we were going to join the peace team that was already there; we hoped our presence would discourage U.S. bombing. "We want to be with the children," Sis said. Mr. Jamal listened for no more than fifteen seconds. "OK," he said. "Give me your passports. Let me see what I can do." With that, the door opened. Even an unjust judge, Jesus said, will eventually grant the persistent widow's request for his own sake. Maybe that's what had happened here. Or maybe God had worked a miracle. Just who Mr. Jamal was or what authority he had to give visas without a letter from the Foreign Ministry was not clear to us. What we did know was that we were going to Baghdad.

"Back to the embassy tomorrow," I had written in my journal the night before. "For the first time, I am hopeful. Should we get the visas, we still have to make a decision [whether we want to go]. But I think we will go. We will go because this is what we came for. We will go if we are called to go on from here." Our decision-making process was short. We would only agree to go if there was consensus in the group that God was still calling us to Baghdad. We went around the circle, each person sharing her or his own sense of the Spirit's leading. We were in agreement. God had called us to go to Iraq at this time, even before we knew the significance of the timing. God had opened a way for us, removing insurmountable obstacles. God would go before us, offering himself as our shield.

God's shield, Jim had said, included the communion of saints— those who live forever, even though they are dead, because their lives have been joined with God's life. A communion of saints, I had learned, would be my traveling companions on the journey through the desert into Iraq. We were not perfect people, nor did we have all the answers to the mess we were driving into. We were, however, committed to the self-giving love that is fundamental to the workings of the universe. Ours was an experiment with Jesus' principle of the seed: "Only if a seed falls into the ground and dies," Jesus said, "can it bring forth life." Every farmer knows this. Still, it is hard to believe until you see it. Activist preacher Jim Wallis likes to say that "hope is believing in spite of the evidence and then watching the evidence change." As we decided to go to Baghdad, the evidence didn't look good. We knew that bombs had already been falling for nearly a week. In terms of effectiveness, we knew that going was not the most strategic thing to do. We weren't going to stop a war that had already started. And we most likely could help more in terms of humanitarian aid after the fighting was over. But our call was to be with those who were suffering—to give them our lives in weakness so that we might see the glory of God's new humanity together. Only with Iraqis could we "watch the evidence change." Choosing to go meant choosing to save our lives by losing them.

Confessing Jesus as Lord, we set out to follow him into the desert. In the city of Amman I had come to see that the politics of the New Jerusalem provide, by God's grace, a real alternative to the politics of this world. The City of God had burst into the life of our little community. The Holy Spirit had descended like a dove, baptizing me into a whole new vision of God's kingdom. From Amman, though, the Spirit was driving us out into the desert. At 2:00 a.m. we loaded into a custom van and a Suburban and drove east from Amman into the night. I still had a lot to learn. But what I needed to see God could show me only in the darkness of the desert.

III.

INTO THE DESERT

F inding drivers who were willing to risk their business and their lives on the road to Baghdad had not been easy. All the Jordanian taxi companies had canceled their service to Iraq, as had the Syrians. (The day before, we'd heard, a bus from Syria was bombed on the road to Baghdad.) Only Iraqis were willing to make the trip through the desert at this point. We were told that two Iraqi brothers were now in Amman and wanted to go home to Baghdad. Their price was four times the going rate. But they were willing to go. Jerry went to find them.

When they returned, Jerry introduced us to Omar and Ahmed, both bulky men who were dressed nicely in GQ fashion. The older of the two was bald, his head shaved slick and waxed. They could have just as easily been hit men as taxi drivers. I was somewhat relieved to learn that Leah and I would be riding with the younger of the two; he wore glasses, seemed a bit looser, and smiled on occasion. We were both delighted that Jim Douglass and Weldon Nisly, a Mennonite pastor from Seattle, would be our traveling companions. Both Jim and Weldon had impressed us with their peaceful presence and quiet confidence in God's providence. Peace and confidence, we suspected, were virtues that would prove helpful on this journey.

Before leaving Amman we had been extremely busy, buying supplies to take with us, making calls to the U.S., and getting out a press release at the Intercontinental Hotel, command-central for the international media covering the Iraq story. I had not slept in nearly twenty-four hours and I was exhausted from the emotional windstorm that had accompanied a long day of activity. As we drove away I watched the lights of Amman fade into the distance behind us and thought about how good it would feel to close my eyes for a few hours and not worry about the road that lay ahead. But I couldn't. Our new friend at the wheel, despite his courage, was nervous. He sped into the darkness, following only the red glow of his brother's taillights in front of us. To calm his nerves Ahmed put in a CD of Arabic techno music and cranked up the volume. Jim, in the passenger's seat beside him, recognized Ahmed's anxiety and began clapping his hands, just slightly off the beat, and bounced up and down in his seat. Not able to communicate with words across the English/Arabic language barrier, Jim still found a way to say, "Don't worry. Everything will be OK." Ahmed laughed and clapped along with him for a few seconds. Seeing that we were still going over seventy miles an hour, Leah encouraged Ahmed with a smile and some very clear gestures to keep his hands on the wheel.

As long as we were on the Jordanian side of the border, we didn't feel like there was very much to worry about. We had to stop a couple of times at military checkpoints where sleepy guards gave us quizzical looks, spoke briefly with Ahmed in Arabic, then waved us on. Only once were we asked to get out and show our passports. The women, one soldier indicated courteously, need not get out in the dark. Before leaving Amman, we had asked some university students we had gotten to know at a little Internet café to help us translate into Arabic a short paragraph describing the purpose of our trip. We'd then made copies with the English on one side and Arabic on the other and given everyone some leaflets to share with soldiers on the road. Unsure of the progress U.S. troops had made in their advance toward Baghdad, we didn't know whether the soldiers we met on the road would speak English or Arabic. To the Jordanian checkpoint guards, we offered the Arabic side of our leaflet. They read it, nodded their heads, and handed it back to us. We were free to go.

By sunrise we made it to the border, where we saw the white tents of the Ruweished refugee camp in the early morning light. We had read in the newspapers that the massive emigration out of Iraq that many had anticipated still had not happened. It was true. All the tents stood empty, like a makeshift ghost town in the desert. We stopped in Ruweished City, used the bathroom, got coffee, and ate breakfast. By 7:30 a.m. we were at the Jordanian side of the border. By 8:00 a.m. we had clearance. The whole process was as smooth as we could have imagined. We were the only people leaving Jordan for Iraq that day.

We crossed the no-man's-land and approached the office of the Iraqi border patrol, where a group of guards were standing around talking. When they read our little leaflet they smiled, welcomed us, and waved us on to the office. We parked in front of an enormous picture of Saddam Hussein, got out, and went inside. The lobby had pictures of Saddam on three different walls: one in the traditional Arabic dress, one in his military uniform, and one in a Western business suit. Leah elbowed me and observed that the Western portrait looked strikingly similar to my dad. (At a party the summer before, a friend of Leah's family had recognized the resemblance between my dad and the Iraqi dictator. Needless to say, Dad was not flattered.) I stepped up to the counter and presented my passport. "You are an American?" the official asked. "You do not look like an American." "Well, actually," I said, "my father looks a lot like your president." He laughed. "You could easily be an Iraqi," he said.

After recording all of our information by hand, the official ushered us into an empty waiting room and served tea while those with electronic equipment were taken to register their possessions in a different office. Cell phones were not allowed, another official told us. "The Americans may hone in on your signal and try to bomb you," he said. The Iraqis, it seemed, were trying to protect us from our own government. U.S. bombs, they knew, were often not very discriminate in their destruction.

As we drove away from the border office, the sides of the road were lined with men sitting on suitcases—seventy-five to one hundred of them. Some waved as if asking for rides. Ahmed stopped to give a couple of bottles of water to a few of them. Although no Iraqis had left the country for the refugee camps on the other side, hundreds, we later learned, had returned to their motherland. The men on the road were waiting for a bus from Baghdad that would take them back to fight for their homes. As we drove further we saw that some of them were not bothering to wait for the bus. They had already started walking the more than three-hundred-mile journey through the desert to Baghdad. On their faces was a look of determination that reminded me of a comment I'd read in the Amman newspaper: "This U.S. 'cowboy culture' will not defeat a culture as rich and deep as that of Iraq."

We had been told in a briefing just before we left Amman that a bridge had been bombed out on the highway about an hour inside the Iraqi border. The only way around it was to bypass that stretch of road by going through a little town called Rutba. It was the first exit we saw off the highway. Rutba was a small town in the middle of the Western desert, the only mark of civilization between the Jordanian border and the outskirts of Baghdad. As we drove through, I peered out the window for my first glimpse of Iraqi life. The streets were relatively busy with people moving about and a long line of cars at the gas station. In the center of town a tanker had been hit with a missile and sat charred in the street. A building marked "Customs" had also been bombed, as had a section of bridge in town. We passed through as quickly as possible, slowing down no more than necessary. Our brothers at the wheel were determined to make it home as quickly as possible.

Back on the highway we began to see more charred vehicles— eerie shells with their doors swung open. It was impossible to say whether the passengers had made it out alive. We passed a bus, not burnt but stopped and empty in the middle of the right lane. Where were the people? And why had they left their bus in the middle of a desert? Further along we passed another bus that had been bombed. Absolutely everything except the metal frame was gone. A growing storm blew dust through the seats where people had been just days before, already beginning to bury their charred remains. Our van rocked back and forth a bit as we sped past at nearly eighty miles per hour.

At one point on the road we saw a car that was still burning on the right shoulder ahead of us. We slowed to pass through the cloud of black smoke and emerged on the other side to see four Iraqi militia-men with their guns on the ground and their hands in the air. On a hill just beside the road, a U.S. Special Forces unit had its guns trained on the men—and now on us. They motioned for us to stop and both drivers did, nervously waiting for further orders. I scanned the hillside: two tanks, two armored personnel carriers, and about ten men holding guns. Leah stared at one man the whole time—a man who was staring back at her through the scope of his M-16.

It was the first time I had ever been on the "other side" of the U.S. military. Weapons that had been developed for my security were not the slightest bit comforting as I looked at them from the receiving end. Just minutes before encountering the troops, Leah had asked Jim if the dust storm we were driving through might keep us from being spotted by planes flying overhead. "They can hit us if they want to," Jim had said matter-of-factly. Seeing the fear on Leah's face, though, he smiled and added, "Remember, God is our shield. He is the only protection we need. God will take care of us." As I looked at the guns aimed toward us, I remembered Jim's words.

Repeating those words over again, I was also reminded of an e-mail I'd received from a Catholic friend named John who works at the Pentagon. Believing in the necessity of truth for the sake of peace-making, our team had decided to be very transparent about our plans to enter Iraq against the orders of the U.S. government. I had sent a copy of our press release explaining the delegation's intentions to John. He could do with it whatever he saw fit, I told him. John's response was short and professional, but I remembered that he had ended it with those very same words: "God will take care of you." Somehow the phrase wasn't as comforting from him as it was when Jim said it.

Hearing the same words said in two very different ways helped me to see more clearly the conflict of realities we found ourselves in. The battle, it seemed, was not only Iraqi versus American. (In a sense it was not that at all. The Iraqis we had just met at the border demon-strated no animosity toward us as Americans.) The fundamental battle was against opposing views of reality. Jim and John did not mean the same things when they said, "God will take care of you," though the distinction was very fine. Neither of them assumed God's care meant we would return safely from the violence of Iraq. After all, thousands of people whom God loves would die (and continue to die) in that conflict. "God will take care of you" seemed to suggest for both of them a sense of abandonment to reality. But there were two different realities: the reality of Christ's kingdom and the reality of the Pentagon. The difference between Jim and John was the eyes with which they each saw the reality we were experiencing.

In the twentieth century, I knew from my study of theology and politics, the American theologian Reinhold Niebuhr had won the imagination of the church in the United States with his doctrine of "Christian Realism." Niebuhr, who had been a vocal pacifist before World War I, looked at the evil of Nazi Germany in World War II and concluded that Christians had a moral obligation to use force in defense of Jews and other citizens of the free world. In an ideal world, Niebuhr taught, we would not have to fight wars. In the real world of sinful people, however, we do. With Niebuhr's logic the American church found it easy to simplify questions of power to a debate between realism and idealism. The young and irresponsible could be idealists, perhaps. But the church would have to be realistic, educated churchmen had thought since Niebuhr. With my new understanding of the reality of the new humanity, I seriously doubted that the reality of Niebuhr's "Christian Realism" was the only option. Even as we looked at the barrels of U.S. guns, Jim had eyes to see another reality.

I, however, could not see so clearly. While I had some good theology under my belt, my spiritual resources were lacking. It was not that I needed to know more. I had studied Scriptural teaching on powers and principalities. I knew that the powers, like us, were created by God and thus good by their nature. We should submit to them, Paul said in Romans 13. At the same time, I knew that the powers are fallen and that, also like us, they often do not honor God as they were made to. Thus, we are sometimes called to struggle against them. "Our struggle is not against flesh and blood," Paul wrote, "but against the authorities, against the cosmic powers of this present darkness, against the spiritual forces of evil in heavenly places." Our struggle is not in vain because we worship the One who has already defeated the powers, unmasking and redeeming them in his death and resurrection.

"Now what these 'cosmic authorities' were in Paul's mind is not easy to say in modern terms," John Yoder had taught me. "They are not human persons. Yet they influence human events and structures. What we call the state, the economy, the media, ideology—they are their instruments."

As we sat in silence, staring back at U.S. troops, I knew that the powers were neither Iraqi nor American, though they worked through governments and individuals in both countries. Saddam was not the demon the U.S. government portrayed him to be, even though he had done some devilish things. Bush was not the incarnation of evil that many in the Arabic world (and in the liberal peace community) made him out to be either. But he was responsible for a great deal of evil. As I was. "If you are angry with a brother or sister," Jesus said, "you will be subject to judgment." If I felt anything in the paralysis of that moment on the road to Baghdad, it was anger. I was not faithful enough to love the U.S. soldier who had his weapon trained on Leah, our friends, and me. The chaos of the desert exposed the dark caverns of my own soul, depths that I did not know and could not understand because I had not faced them seriously before. What I could see was this: there is a difference between understanding theology and being transformed by God in our inner depths. The latter is required to see the reality that Jim could see. The desert had exposed my blindness.

The conversion I was having on the road to Baghdad, I later realized, was the same thing Jerry had experienced during his year of solitary confinement in another desert. What he had not been able to find chasing the latest news story found him in the darkness of his cell. It reminded me of the saying from the Desert Father, Abba Moses: "Stay in your cell, and your cell will teach you everything." My rearing in evangelical churches had not taught me the importance of contemplative prayer or silence. Prayer was important, I had learned as a child, but it was about praising God, confessing my sins, thanking God for his forgiveness, and asking him to save others. We even had an acronym: A for adoration, C for confession, T for thanksgiving, and S for supplication. These were the ACTS of prayer. I had learned them well. Our journey into the desert, however, was pushing me to see that there is more to prayer. And, perhaps more importantly, there is less.

A newsman once asked Mother Teresa what she said to God when she prayed. "I don't say anything, I listen," she replied. "OK... and what does God say?" the newsman inquired further. "He doesn't say anything. He listens." At a moment when activism offered me no answers, my own weakness helped me see the importance of contemplation. Contemplation, the spiritual masters teach us, is about abandoning oneself to God in silence. It is to become less so that Jesus can become more. Without it, there is little hope of ever becoming the kind of people who can see the reality of God's kingdom and practice the politics of Jesus. With it, our active lives find the center they need.

Jesus turned to contemplation for his own spiritual direction. Often, the gospels tell us, Jesus would steal away and pray by himself on a mountainside. The kingdom of God in the gospels is proclaimed out of the desert—out of Jesus's solitude in the wilderness. How had I not seen this before? Contemplation was the spiritual center of Jesus's life and ministry. Mark's gospel says that it was the Spirit of God himself who drove Jesus out into the wilderness. The verb Mark uses is the very same one that is used when Jesus "drives out" the money-changers from his Father's house. The desert is certainly not a place where anyone goes naturally. It is not easy. But it is essential. For the desert is where Jesus confronts the powers face to face. Satan himself, the prince of demons, meets Jesus in his solitude. This is by no means a "quiet time," carefully planned to reduce stress and restore peace of mind. It is the furthest thing from it. Jesus goes into the desert to fight. Here he wins the first battle in the war of the Lamb.

"He was with the wild beasts and the angels ministered to him." For those with eyes to see, Mark has described a spiritual battlefield. "Wild beasts," in the language of the prophet Daniel, are the spiritual forces behind the kingdoms of this world (Dan. 7). Alone in the desert, Jesus faces the powers head on. Here he is closer to the root of evil than he would be before Pilate or Caesar. Mark makes this point clear in his telling of the story. As Ched Myers observes in his *Binding the Strong Man*, Jesus's first direct action campaign against the evil of the temple establishment was not in Jerusalem but in the desert. Here he gets at the heart of the matter. To begin in Jerusalem or Rome might mistakenly suggest that the fundamental problem with humanity is political. Not so, Jesus says. Beneath the corruption of politics and the oppression of economics, the lies of the media and the perversion of bigotry, the dysfunction of families and the neuroses of individuals— beneath all of these manifestations of evil lies the same spiritual root. To confront it we need only to look honestly at the darkness within each of us. "The heart is devious above all else; it is perverse," Jeremiah confessed. "Who can understand it?" Contemplation is an intentional effort to practice what I was experiencing for a moment in the desert of Iraq: to look into the darkness of one's own heart and see the whole world go black, like Jerusalem on Good Friday.

I am convinced that Jesus went to the cross because he had disciplined himself to go to the desert. The radical faith that his action required was rooted in his spiritual discipline of contemplation. "When God is about to justify a man, he damns him," Martin Luther said. And it is true, even for the Son of God. "My God, my God, why have you forsaken me?" Jesus cries from the cross. In the utter weakness of death, God's power is made manifest in resurrection. Jesus wins the battle once again through willing submission to the principalities and powers of the cosmos, in obedience to his Father. His active obedience, however, is only possible because he is disciplined in abandoning himself to God. This was what God had brought me out into the desert to see.

I do not know how long we sat there staring at the troops. But all of a sudden they began waving us on. Ahmed hesitated, checking to make sure that he understood their directions. With the cannon of a tank and several machine guns pointed at us, he didn't want to make any mistakes. Once the command to leave was clear, however, he wasted no time. Our van took off, and I looked out the rear window to see the Iraqi militiamen on the road running toward us. As my eyes were being opened to the importance of the contemplative life, it seemed the Iraqi militiamen had received a revelation of their own: here was a potential getaway vehicle. Realizing this, the U.S. soldiers had decided it was best to move us out of the situation. I watched the troops from both sides fade into the dust as Ahmed sped forward. Then, I heard the Arabic techno come on again. It blasted from the speakers in the van like a great sigh of relief. Ahmed was laughing, happy to still be alive, no doubt. Jim began clapping and bouncing in his seat again. Before, it had been a way for him to say that everything was going to be OK. This time, it was a prayer of thanksgiving, I think. God had been our shield.

We did not drive more than twenty minutes before encountering another set of troops, all Iraqi this time. We were relieved. They stopped us at a makeshift checkpoint, asked Ahmed a question in Arabic, read our little paper describing the purpose of our mission, and smiled. "Very good," one soldier said in English. We were free to go. The difference between this encounter and the one we had just had with the Americans was striking. Our own fellow Americans, frightened as we were in a desert we knew little about, had been our enemy. The gulf across which they had pointed their guns at us was no more than twenty yards wide. But it was a distance not one of us was prepared to cross. Had we been able to talk together, what would we have said? The enemy troops, on the other hand, were not threatening to us at all. Across a language barrier, just minutes from enemy lines, we connected. "Very good," the soldier had said. It was both an affirmation and a word of welcome from one who had every reason to believe that Americans had worn out their welcome on Iraqi soil. The line between "us" and "them" blurred as we realized that we could trust the Iraqis more than we could the Americans.

Crossing the battle line, we realized how close the American and Iraqi troops were to one another (and how close the troops were now to Baghdad). Beyond the checkpoint we began to see more Iraqis—some in uniform, some in civilian clothes—running toward where we had come from with guns in their hands. The dust storm was getting worse. Most of the men held one arm in front of their face as they ran to take their place on the front lines of the coming battle. We stopped for another checkpoint, and watched as a Suburban pulled up behind us. Its rear windows had been shot out, the Iraqi driver told us, by the same U.S. troops that we had encountered just minutes before him on the road. When the soldiers had motioned for him to stop, he hadn't. It had nearly cost him his life. The car in front of us on the road, then, had been blown up just minutes before our arrival on the scene. The car behind us had been fired on by the U.S. troops, losing its rear windows. Somehow we had passed through without harm.

On the outskirts of Baghdad we began to see oil fires burning. As a way of covering the city with a cloud and decreasing visibility for the Americans, Iraqis had opened oil spouts all around the city and set them on fire. The dark black smoke that billowed out mixed with clouds of dust that were still blowing across the landscape. Often we could not see more than a few dozen yards in front of us. At points when we drove through the oil smoke, we could see nothing at all. Still, as we approached the city there was a fair amount of traffic on the highway. The sight of others driving about was reassuring. No longer were we the only car on the road still moving. We had returned to civilization.

On a street off to the side of the highway, a group of kids was playing soccer. Did they not care that dust was blowing in their eyes as they passed the ball to one another? Did they not know that their country was being invaded by an enemy that was just miles away? These children were used to hardship, we knew. Yet still, they were able to play. In a field just off to our right, I saw a man on a tractor, plowing the earth. He was preparing to plant for another year. No doubt, he knew he was living in the middle of a war. But life goes on, he seemed to say with his action. Fields must get plowed. The war would end at some point. But the cycle of plowing, planting, harvesting, and plowing again would go on. Close to the ground, one Iraqi farmer could see that. In their F-16 fighters far above us, I was fairly certain that the U.S. pilots could not.

Nor could they see from above that Baghdad was a beautiful city. Clearly European in design, its wide avenues and large traffic circles reminded me of Paris. Only at the center of every circle was a statue of Saddam. As it had been at the immigration office, his image was every-where. Maps were not allowed in Iraq (as they could be used to plan an attack), so I found it hard to get my bearings. I could see a river and knew that it must be either the Tigris or Euphrates, those ancient streams of life that had been the basis for more than one great civilization. The Garden of Eden, some had postulated, was planted between these two rivers. Babylon, that great city of old, was founded here.

When we arrived, though, the city was broken. It had by then suffered seven days of bombing. The palaces and government buildings had almost all been hit. The grandeur of an empire was ruined. Coming out of the desert into such a city, I could see better the connection between our spiritual and political problem as human beings. Though God started the human story in a garden, a garden that might have not been far from this place, I knew from Revelation that God meant for our story to culminate in a city—a city that descends from heaven, no less. That city, the New Jerusalem, is a political reality that Jesus has initiated in his kingdom. Only God can bring it down from heaven, but we who are called to live as Christ's body, the new temple, have been given power to practice the politics of Jesus in this world. That power, however, is something we must go to the desert to receive. It is not enough to know that it exists. The Spirit drives us out into the wilderness of contemplation to transform us into a new humanity that lives by the power of the cross. With new eyes, we see a different reality. Ours is a whole new world. "Behold," Paul says, "new creation!"

Having passed through the desert, I could begin to read the Scriptures with new eyes. "What did you go out into the desert to see," Jesus asks a crowd after teaching them about the kingdom of God and showing them what God's reign looks like by healing the sick and raising the dead. John the Baptist's disciples, having heard and seen this good news, rush to tell John about "all these things." John sends them back with a question: "Are you the one who is to come or should we expect someone else?" As the scene unfolds, John is helping us ask the central question: Is Jesus really the long-awaited Messiah? Is he the Servant of the Lord who will overthrow the unjust kingdoms of this world and establish the reign of God?

For a Jew in first-century Palestine, there could have been no more important question than the one John was asking. To John's disciples Jesus responds, "Go tell him what you've seen and heard." That is, go tell him that the reality of God's kingdom is at hand. The New Jerusalem is upon us. Jesus' words and deeds together proclaim that a new political era has begun. To the crowds, however, Jesus asks this question: "What did you go out into the desert to see?"

Why did the people of Jerusalem leave the safety of city walls and Roman soldiers to go out into the desert and hear John the Baptist's message? Was it just for the show, Jesus asks rhetorically—to see a "reed swayed by the wind" or a "man dressed in fine clothes"? No, there was something more than a thrill-seeking crowd and a crowd-pleasing showman out in that desert. A revolution was beginning with John's message of repentance and the people's recognition of John as a prophet. His baptism was reinitiating them into the common life that God had given Israel in the desert centuries before, when he had led them with a cloud by day and a fire by night. To be free from the bondage of Pharaoh (i.e., the power of Empire), they had to pass through the desert again.

"If you are willing," Jesus says, "then this one is Elijah," the great prophet who is to return and make a way for the coming of the Lord. If you believe, the kingdom of God is among you. The true revolution has finally come. "Among those born of women there is no one greater than John; yet the one who is least in the kingdom of God is greater than he." The kingdom that John announces and Jesus embodies is a true revolution in that it turns the whole world upside down—or, better said, right-side up again. The poor are made rich, the rich poor. The last shall be first in this kingdom. Whoever would save his life must lose it.

What did you go out into the desert to see?

The answer is a revolution.

Jesus knew this because he had himself gone out into the desert. After hearing John's message and receiving his baptism, Jesus was thrown by the Spirit into the wilderness. For forty days and nights he fasted and prayed, wrestling with the devil's temptations. "All the options laid before Jesus by the tempter are ways of being king," John Yoder writes. In Luke's telling, the ways of being king are presented as first economic, then political, and finally religious.

The temptation to turn stones to bread is an opportunity to win the favor of the masses. If you feed them, they will follow you, the devil suggests. Indeed, this is what happens when Jesus feeds the five thousand. They want to make him king. The devil's offer of all the kingdoms in the world is a more obvious temptation to seize the throne. But the religious option is perhaps the most tempting. For the long-awaited Messiah is a religious hope. And that may well have been the only hope Jesus's contemporaries had left. "Christianity arose in a re-mote and poverty-stricken region of the vast Roman Empire, among the struggling farm families of a frontier province that could only be classified as 'chronically underdeveloped' by modern economic crite-ria," write Richard Horsley and Niel Silberman in their book, *The Message and the Kingdom*. This is the social context from which Jesus goes out into the desert.

Political discontent ran high in first-century Palestine as the Jews suffered exploitation by the Roman powers and capitulation by their own leadership. All three forms of power that Jesus faces in the desert are very real options that could lead to a liberation movement. Yet, while Jesus sees the need for liberation clearly, he rejects the ways of the devil to espouse a different movement—the kingdom of God.

"The time has come," Jesus proclaims in Mark's gospel. "The king-dom of God is near." Jesus returns from the desert to announce a new political era. "At the heart of this movement," Horsley and Silberman explain, "was the dream of a down-to-earth Kingdom first enunciated by the prophets of the tiny land of Israel several hundred years before: 'They shall build homes and inhabit them; they shall plant vineyards and eat their fruit. They shall not build and another inhabit; they shall not plant and another eat. For like the days of a tree shall the days of my people be, and my chosen shall long enjoy the work of their hands' (Isa. 65:21-22)."

Jesus, what did you go out into the desert to see?

The kingdom of God—a revolution.

But more, for Jesus successfully rejects the temptation to liberate his people by force when he turns down the devil's powers. What Jesus sees in the desert is more than a vision of the kingdom that is to be; it is a fundamentally radical way to get there. In Amman I had been able to see what the New Jerusalem could look like. In Baghdad I could see the destruction wrought by the politics of this world. Only in the desert, however, could I see my own need for a spiritual conversion. With Jesus in the desert, I had begun to see the need for a heart that can embrace the cross.

The way of suffering love, Jesus knows, is the only way to overcome the power of sin that is the real root of Israel's oppression and Rome's arrogance—Saddam's evil empire and America's unjust warmaking. You cannot buy freedom from sin. You cannot win it in war. You can't even grasp it with religious fervor. But you can embrace it in love. To embrace freedom in the face of evil is necessarily to suffer. Yet, in the vulnerability of suffering—in the harsh elements of the desert—we find the mercy of a God who gives himself in love. In the desert I could see the cross on which Jesus was crucified for my sin. The cross was not only a window into a new kind of politics. It was an instrument of death for which I was responsible. As a peacemaker I had thought I could simply embrace the cross and follow the way of Jesus. But the problem was not so simple. For in my sin I also used the cross to crucify Jesus. The powers I sought to fight against in global politics were powers that had rooted themselves inside of me. Yet, as I stood before the cross in my role of crucifier, I could hear Christ's words, "Father, forgive them for they know not what they do." Despite my sin, God loved me. He loved me at my wretched worst. In that love I could see a way toward the new humanity.

In the late fourth century, as Christianity entered the mainstream after the Roman Emperor Constantine extended favors to the church, there was another movement of Christians into the desert. Forsaking the security of their Roman cities, these early monastics and hermits abandoned themselves to God so they might learn from him in their vulnerability what it means to love. In her book *To Love as God Loves*, church historian Roberta Bondi observes, "One reason the monastics left ordinary life in their own culture was that they were trying to establish a new model where everyone was on the same footing, where loving service was the model for everybody." They were trying to rediscover the original revolution that Jesus had gone out into the desert to see. They wanted to practice the kingdom of God as an alternative to the powers of Empire. But they knew that the desert was the only way to get there.

"How can one close one's eyes to the fact that the demons themselves have taken over rule of the world?" Dietrich Bonhoeffer had asked in 1932. "It is the powers of darkness who have here made an awful conspiracy." The same could be said as I looked at the streets of Baghdad. Seeing the destruction as a conspiracy of spiritual powers, though, gave me reason to hope. For the same God who had been our shield on the road to Baghdad had also promised that the power of love could defeat these forces. Would our love be enough to stop the U.S. military? I felt confident enough to pray for such a miracle. I had come to Baghdad to show love. But I still didn't know what love meant. Fortunately, I'd come to the right place to learn.

IV.

BY THE WATERS OF BABYLON

Peggy Gish met us on the sidewalk outside Al Dar, the little hotel where CPT was based in Baghdad. She was wearing a black shirt with white lettering that said, "NO WAR," and the red CPT hat that marks Christian peacemakers in conflict zones around the world. Peggy had been in Baghdad since the previous October, working closely with the Sisters of Charity's home for children and getting to know her neighbors around the Dar, which was located in a residential district of Baghdad. She was happy to welcome us into what had become her home.

Carrying our bags through the storm that continued to blow dust in our faces, we followed Peggy into the lobby of the hotel. The rest of the CPT team was there to greet us, along with the staff of the Dar. Our relief finally to be there was matched by their relief to see us arrive safely. From communication with CPT's Chicago office, they had known that we were coming, but only knew rumors about the conditions of the road and the position of soldiers along it. What they did know was that bombs had been falling for nearly a week and a dust storm was raging outside. Had they been in our position, they would never have come, they told us. But they were delighted to see us alive. "We've had no bombing in Baghdad today," Peggy said to us. "The people are saying that they have never seen a dust storm like this one before. 'Allah is protecting us,' they say." God had certainly protected us.

Leah and I had been disappointed when we first learned that we would have to stay in a hotel in Baghdad. "If we're going to Iraq to be with the people," we asked, "shouldn't we try to stay with them in their homes?" Those who were much more informed than us about the history of the Peace Team in Iraq told us that scores of people in Baghdad would certainly be more than willing to open their homes to us. And all of the peacemakers would love to stay in Iraqi homes (as CPT often does, for example, in the West Bank or Colombia). Doing so under Saddam's government, however, was nearly impossible. It would make the Foreign Ministry officials suspicious of what we were doing behind closed doors. And it would put the families in far too much danger. CPT had settled, then, for a small hotel in a residential neighborhood. The only other guests were a pair of freelance Japanese photographers.

While we were eager to share with our CPT friends about the harrowing journey through the desert, they made it clear that we should not say too much. We were being watched. "Saddam's eyes and ears are everywhere," they told us. And they were very willing to explain in the hearing of those ears their position on the matter. Lisa Martens, another member of the permanent team, told us that CPT was committed to not aiding Iraqi or American intelligence in this war. We would not make it easier for either side to commit its violence. So, she advised, we should not talk about what we saw when encountering the troops on the road to Baghdad nor where exactly we had seen them. We were here to be a peaceful presence and to witness the suffering of the Iraqi people. We could save our storytelling for later.

While the team was adamant in its refusal to cooperate with the violence of Saddam's regime, we also saw quickly that every relationship mattered in this peacemaking project. Mr. Sayd, the Iraqi Foreign Ministry officer assigned to watch the CPT team, stopped by the hotel shortly after our arrival. Lisa introduced us to him as a friend and told us how the team had visited with his family on their farm outside of Baghdad. Mr. Sayd greeted us and offered figs that he had brought with him from the farm. He smiled and listened carefully as we introduced ourselves and explained why we had come to Baghdad. After thanking us, Mr. Sayd gave us a report on the day's events. "Civilian deaths have now passed five hundred," he said. "This morning my son came to me and said, 'Bring me a gun so I can fight.'" He told us he had heard about a videotape one of us had made on the road to Baghdad and asked to see it. Lisa spoke up again, saying that we didn't have anything we were willing to share. Mr. Sayd nodded and did not pursue the issue any further. He respected the team's position. But it was also clear that he had received a report on our conversation prior to his arrival.

Leah and I were anxious to ask the whereabouts of our good friend Shane Claiborne from Philadelphia who had already been in Baghdad for a couple of weeks with an organization called Voices in the Wilderness ("Voices," for short). Voices was CPT's partner organization that had been in Baghdad since its founder, Kathy Kelly, traveled to Iraq shortly after the first Gulf War and began documenting the effects of that war and the economic sanctions that followed it. Voices and CPT together made up the Iraq Peace Team (IPT), the only internationals other than sequestered reporters and some human shields who had stayed in Baghdad after the bombing started. Most of Voices' people were staying at a larger hotel, Al Fanar, which was within walking distance. Shane, we were told, would be joining us for dinner.

The team cooked its own meals at the Dar, each member taking a turn in the kitchen. That first night we had a wonderful vegetable stew and some bread from a local bakery. It felt so good to eat after our long day on the road that I had to remind myself that resources were limited and I should practice restraint. At the end of the meal, though, there were still some leftovers. I was glad to finish them off. We had a wonderful time catching up with Shane over dinner, listening to his stories from his time there before and after the bombs started. He was particularly troubled that night by an interview he had had with a U.S. reporter on the telephone. On the air the reporter had asked him why he hated America so much that he had left his home to go live with the enemy. "Why does loving Iraqis mean you hate America?" Shane asked. He had been in Baghdad long enough to be surprised by the reporter's question. The telephone line that connected Baghdad to New York was a reminder that we and our friends back home were living in different worlds.

Part of our orientation to this strange new world of a war zone was a tour of the makeshift bomb shelter the team had made on the first floor of the hotel. We all had rooms on the second floor, they told us, but if things got bad at night, we were welcome to come to this room on the first floor where all the windows had been boarded over and there was a supply of food and water. "Just bring your pillow down with you if you'd feel better sleeping here," Peggy said. Almost no one had used the shelter yet, but they knew things might get worse as the U.S. and British troops got closer to Baghdad. As it was, the team had grown accustomed to sleeping through the bombing in their own rooms. But things were always changing now.

It had been more than forty-eight hours since we had slept. Leah and I were eager to lie down anywhere we could. A young man at the desk gave us the key to our room and we climbed the stairs to find that, as the young married couple, we'd been given the honeymoon suite. As a joke Shane had told the CPT team we were just married and had decided to honeymoon in Baghdad. The room was much nicer than our bedroom at home in Philadelphia. I opened a window, as we had been instructed, to keep the glass from shattering if a bomb fell close by in the night. We brushed our teeth together, and I collapsed onto the bed as Leah finished changing into her pajamas. We heard a rumble, like thunder, and then another—this time closer. The doors on the dresser across the room rattled. "Should we go downstairs?" Leah asked. I heard her, but couldn't answer. My body was exhausted.

Leah got in bed beside me and turned off the light before the next blast. I felt it pass through my body like a wave as the floor shook beneath me. Leah, who grew up in California, said it felt like an earthquake. It was time to go downstairs, she said. But I couldn't make my body move. Leah opened the door to see if others were going downstairs. There was no one in the hallway. She walked down to the front desk where a couple of young guys were watching television and smoking cigarettes. Not knowing how much English, if any, they spoke, Leah asked simply, "Everything OK?"

"OK. No problem," they said, holding a thumb up and smiling. Leah was not convinced. She returned to the room, asking again if I thought we should go downstairs. I'm not sure what I thought about her question, but I remember wanting to say something and not finding the strength to open my mouth. I could hear Leah, but I couldn't say anything. I couldn't even think. Leah swears that after the next series of blasts, as she insisted that we leave the room, I said to her, "Maybe it's just the wind." I don't remember saying it. But I don't remember very much at all from that night—only the deep, sick feeling in my stomach that, no matter how hard I tried, I couldn't do anything. It was the same feeling I'd had in a recurring dream when I was playing basketball in high school. In the dream I ran toward the goal for a breakaway layup. There were no obstacles before me. It looked like an easy two points. Then, as I planted my foot to jump toward the goal, my body went limp and I fell to the floor. It was a manifestation of my worst fear in high school. In Baghdad, now, it was a reality.

I remember Leah standing over me, crying. "Please wake up, Jonathan, you're scaring me," she said. Somehow, her tears brought me back. I was able to connect with reality and get my body to stand up. Still, I don't think I said anything. We walked together to the bomb shelter room downstairs and lay down for our first night in Baghdad. Leah says it took her hours to fall asleep as she listened to the bombs that continued to fall intermittently in the night. I don't even remember closing my eyes.

When I woke up the next morning it was quiet. I climbed the stairs to our room and took a shower. Halfway into it I realized that the water was hot. "Wait," I thought. "We didn't even have hot water in Amman." Here I was in the middle of a war zone taking a hot shower in the honeymoon suite of a quaint little hotel. Just miles away, people had lost their homes and even their lives in the night. Meanwhile, I was washing my hair, feeling quite refreshed after a good night's sleep. The irony was bitter.

After breakfast we had an orientation with two permanent members of IPT, Neville Watson and Cathy Breen. Neville greeted us with a story about a man who was dying and went to Jesuit priest and peace activist Daniel Berrigan for counsel. "I've just learned that I'm dying," he said to Father Dan. "My, that must be very exciting," Dan replied. "So," Neville said to us, "you've come to Baghdad at a very exciting time."

Both Neville and Cathy were honest about the fact that IPT's role, like almost everything in Iraq, was uncertain. Rules changed by the day as the Iraqi government scrambled to maintain a sense of control, while its top leaders fled into hiding and those left tried to pretend that everything was OK. "You must understand that Iraq is a control society," Cathy said. Despite the fact that most of their official buildings had been destroyed, government officials refused to acknowledge defeat. And they felt responsible for IPT's safety. Rules were getting tighter. It had become increasingly difficult to travel freely in the city, and no one from IPT was allowed to be out after dark anymore. All of this affected the team's mission, of course. Hospital and house visits were monitored by foreign ministry officials. We could only travel in approved taxis. Neville admitted that he had been opposed to our coming into the situation at this point. Just getting to Baghdad had been dangerous enough. Now we had to try to learn the rules and find our place in the team's mission at a time when everything was in flux. He had argued against our coming. Now that we were here, however, he had come to greet us. We had a lot to learn, and we needed to learn it fast.

One of the lessons that Voices in the Wilderness had stressed since coming to Iraq in the early nineties was the disastrous effect of the U.S.-backed economic sanctions against Iraq. We got a quick lesson in how the Iraqi economy had been destroyed over the past thirteen years. We were each handed a stack of two hundred fifty dinar bills. Before the first Gulf War in 1991, they told us, each of these bills was worth more than three hundred dollars. Now, they were each worth less than eight cents. The stack in our hand would buy us lunch at a restaurant on the street, but nothing more. I didn't have to think long to imagine the effect of such a cataclysmic change in a nation's economy. No matter how much money someone had before the sanctions, it was worth next to nothing now. Furthermore, no amount of money could buy a long list of things that were against the sanctions, including many medical supplies and pencils. The United Nations had attempted to control a dictator by starving the people of his country. It had not worked. Now those same people were living through what the U.S. government had called a "shock and awe" campaign of bombing.

On our first day in Baghdad, however, there was no bombing. Through the windows of the hotel we could see an orange glow, almost like the light at sunset on a crisp fall day. By this time, though, it was noon. We looked out the window onto a strange scene in which everything was a shade of amber. It was as if the windows had been tinted orange, except that when we walked outside nothing changed. Everything still looked the same. The dust from yesterday's storm and the smoke from the oil fires had combined with drastically increased humidity to produce a surreal scene on the streets of Baghdad. Everyone we talked to said they had never seen anything like it before. Whereas the bombs had hardly phased the locals, the weather left them both shocked and awestruck. It was suddenly not as hard for me to visualize those apocalyptic texts in Scripture where the moon turns red and a third of the world goes dark and the rivers turn to blood. It was happening before my eyes. As we walked to a meeting at Al Fanar, drops of mud began to rain down on us in the streets of Baghdad. Had we come to the end of the world?

Our first meeting with IPT was hardly apocalyptic. As we introduced ourselves to one another, I could sense that those who had been here a while were not seeing the day's events with nearly the same intensity I was. They were concerned about logistics, team dynamics, and reports from around the city. A group would discuss options for what to do when the U.S. troops arrived in Baghdad. It could happen any day, they thought. The bizarre reality that was Baghdad under siege had become normal to the thirty-five people who sat around our circle. That thought itself astounded me.

As we walked back to the Dar along the banks of the Tigris River, I recalled the words of Psalm 137 that I had learned to sing as a kid to a tune in a minor key: "By the waters/ the waters/ of Babylon/ we sat down and wept/ and wept…." It was a song that would recur to me over and again during our time in Baghdad. That ancient song of exile gave words to my mourning as I walked the streets of ancient Babylon, a citizen of the world's greatest Babylon, witnessing the destruction that Empire brings. When I could not cry tears of my own, I repeated those words: "By the waters of Babylon, we sat down and wept."

The next day we traveled to Al Shaab market in north Baghdad. The street was busy with both cars and people who had come to examine the damage from two missiles that had hit the market the day before. On the left side of the street there was an apartment building, the front of which had been torn off by the blast. On the right side we saw the remains of a garage, a bakery, and a grocery store. A Sudanese man who had lived in Baghdad for twenty years offered to translate for me. I asked a couple of people what they knew about the residents of the apartment building. One man said that a pregnant woman who was home alone had been killed. Fifteen people had died; fifty were wounded. As we walked the street we came upon a car that had been hit by one of the missiles. The couple in the car had been thrown across the street and the car itself was a pile of charred metal. One man bent over to pick up a copy of the Koran that was lying in the rubble. It was open to a page, part of which had not been burnt in the flames. Someone asked the man to read it aloud. "In that safe country…" he said. Then he started to cry.

By the waters of Babylon, we sat down and wept.

We visited the house of a family that was shattered when a bomb exploded outside their home the night before. A neighbor told us how the mother, father, and son of the family had been sprayed by pellets and glass fragments when a blast broke their second floor window while they were watching TV. We walked out on their roof and looked at the walls around the window, pockmarked with little holes. Charlie Litkey, a Vietnam veteran who won the Congressional Medal of Honor, dug in one of the holes until he found the cube of metal that had penetrated the surface. He and another veteran identified the source of the pellet immediately: a fragmentation bomb. The sight brought back a flood of memories for them.

During the conflict in Indochina, the United States developed fragmentation bombs to maim guerilla fighters so that each victim would have to be carried out of battle by two other men. The idea was to achieve maximum reduction of enemy troops for each hit. It was a textbook case of military efficiency. The veterans with us in Baghdad had seen the often indiscriminate devastation these weapons brought to the people of Vietnam, Cambodia, and Laos. For them, the sight of a cubic metal pellet was a haunting déjà vu.

Prior to and during Operation Iraqi Freedom, the Pentagon insisted that its superior technology could be used in "surgical strikes" to remove strategic military targets. Yes, there would be minimal civilian casualties, they admitted. But only as "collateral damage." This was to be America's most efficient overthrow in history. But as we stood on the roof of a family whose life had been wrecked by a fragmentation bomb, I saw the deep tragedy of our efficiency. "Collateral damage" looked much worse than it sounds in a news report. Outside the house we gathered to take notes on what we had seen. As we were standing there quietly, an elderly woman approached Dave, another member of our team, and began questioning him in Arabic. Though Dave did not speak Arabic, he listened to her attentively. As she talked, her voice grew louder and more staccato in rhythm. She was yelling at Dave and weeping over the destruction of her home. Some of the Iraqi men who were standing there hugged the woman respectfully and tried to comfort her. Her outburst had been an expression of the grief we could all feel.

By the waters of Babylon, we sat down and wept.

The evening after we discovered the remnants of fragmentation bombs buried in the walls of a civilian home, Leah and I visited Al Yarmouk Hospital in Baghdad. I had the chance to ask the head of the emergency room how many patients he had seen with small pellets in their flesh. "Thirty to forty in the past ten days," he said. "The pieces are too small to remove, so we leave them in." The doctor took us to the surgery floor and introduced us to some of the patients. There we met a family with two children injured, a boy and a girl. The girl looked as if she had measles from a distance, but when we came closer I could see that the scabs on her face and neck were from small penetration wounds. Her doctor held up an X-ray to show us the little pieces still inside her body—the same square pellets we had picked out of the wall the day before. As I shook my head in disbelief, the child's mother handed me a picture of her third child, another daughter. This one had not survived, the doctor explained. I put my right hand on my chest and said the few words of Arabic I knew: *Asif jeded*. I'm so sorry.

On our way out of the hospital, the doctor stopped to introduce us to a young man with a bandage on his head. The man extended his hand and shook mine only lightly. I looked in his eyes but felt like he was looking through me, almost as if I were not there. As we walked away the doctor told us the young man's story. Just before the bombing had started, he had been married in Baghdad. He and his wife were worried about worsening conditions in the city, so they went south to a farm for their honeymoon. There a missile had hit the small house where they were staying one night. The young man had wakened to find his young bride decapitated beside him. I thought about how Leah and I were in the honeymoon suite at Al Dar, still taking hot showers. And I felt sick.

By the waters of Babylon, we sat down and wept.

We drove through Baghdad to the Amariya district to visit a bomb shelter that had been hit on the thirteenth of February in 1991. Two bombs, each weighing four thousand pounds, had been dropped on the shelter, breaking through the reinforced concrete and steel that was designed to protect civilians from bombs in the Iran/Iraq war. The U.S. government had said in 1991 that it thought the Iraqi military was hiding munitions inside the shelter. When the second bomb broke through the protective covering of the shelter, the temperature inside immediately rose to four hundred degrees Fahrenheit, killing 408 people inside. Fourteen people had survived, only because they were sleeping in the doorway to the shelter and were blown into the street by the blast.

A guide walked us through the underground shelter, pointing out the places where we could see the outlines of people's bodies that had been burnt into the walls. She showed us a place where we could see the image of a mother, holding her baby against her chest. She pointed to another outline of a hand on which we could see that there had been an engagement ring. Because the shelter was equipped with bathrooms and showers, it had a boiler that had also exploded when the second bomb hit. Boiling water, then, had washed over the people's bodies as they were baking. We could see places where human hair and skin were still stuck to the walls. "There's no difference between this and the Holocaust," Sis Levin exclaimed. The difference, our guide explained calmly, is that no U.S. official had ever apologized for this atrocity. Only at the end of our tour, after she had left, did we learn that our guide had lost her own daughter in Al Amariya shelter.

By the waters of Babylon, we sat down and wept.

Our days in Baghdad were difficult emotionally. Past and present destruction blended into one as the Iraqi people told us their story of America—an America that had made their life hell. We heard the same question repeated by a hundred different mouths: "Why is your country doing this?" We told the Iraqi people how we had tried to discourage our President from going to war. "Isn't America a democracy?" one man asked. Democracy, I tried to explain, is a complicated thing. We had no good answers for most of the questions Iraqis asked us on the streets. Still, they were wonderfully forgiving: "We love Americans," they would often say. "We wish you had a better government, but we love Americans." The Iraqi people, more than anyone in the world, perhaps, understood what it meant to have a government that did its own will. They understood that we could not change our government, but that we had come to be with them as they were suffering. As we walked the streets they greeted us with the standard Arabic salutation: *Salaam*—Peace. Jamil, our friend at the hotel in Amman, had been right: "If you are there with them when the bombs are falling, they will understand."

Not only did they understand. They welcomed us with open arms. One man apologized that his shop was not open. "If it were I would have you in for tea," he said. Middle Eastern hospitality was stronger than any enmity that our governments had produced between Iraqis and Americans. The hospitality reminded me of the politics of the New Jerusalem I was experiencing within our CPT team. Our little community, it seemed, was expanding to include the enemy. More than any of us, however, they were driving the expansion by their radical reception of us, their enemy. I recalled another line from Psalm 137: "If I forget you, O Jerusalem, let my right hand wither! Let my tongue cling to the roof of my mouth, if I do not set Jerusalem above my highest joy."

Remembering was the difficult work we had been called here to do. None of us knew how long we would be able to stay in Baghdad, but we had no plans to leave. Our growing sense among the CPT team was that the most important thing we could do as long as the bombing continued was to memorialize the dead—to remember their lives as sacred gifts from God, the loss of which was a loss to all humanity. We began to conceive of a first-response funeral team. We did not have the resources to care for the dead and wounded in Baghdad. What we could do, though, was go and mourn publicly with those who were left behind. We would not conduct a funeral service. Instead, we would carry a banner that said, in Arabic, "We mourn your dead, ask for forgiveness, and pray to God for peace." We would, perhaps, absorb some anger, as Dave had done from the elderly woman the day before. We would grieve with those who were grieving, making a space to remember. We would symbolically resist the bombs that continued to fall by refusing to fear them. We would fight against the forces of evil behind all this destruction by praying. It was, in the end, all that we could do. Only God could save us.

I went to bed convinced that we had found a faithful role to play in a ludicrous drama that could only get better by ending. We would refuse to forget Jerusalem, our highest joy, by refusing to fear the forces of evil and refusing to forget the lives that were lost. We would go to bomb sites as soon as we could get there. But we would only go to pray. An activism that proclaims the new humanity, then, would be combined with contemplation of our most horrendous evil, man's destruction of man. It was a way that I could walk prayerfully in Baghdad as I continued to sing Psalm 137 over and over in my mind.

By the waters of Babylon, we sat down and wept.

When a bomb woke me up early the next morning, it was the last verse of Psalm 137 that came to mind: "O daughter of Babylon, doomed to destruction, happy is he who repays you for what you have done to us—he who seizes your infants and dashes them against the rocks." I was angry. "Dammit," I grumbled. And I meant it. "Damn those bombs and damn the idiots who keep dropping them." The "daughter of Babylon, doomed to destruction," I was quite certain, was whoever kept dropping those bombs. Not having slept very well in days, I was annoyed. But I was filled with righteous indignation as well. Did the Pentagon realize the psychological effect of constant bombing on a city full of human beings? Did they care that their concentration of bombs during the hours that most people sleep was a diabolical strategy to paralyze a people? Did they know what this was doing to children in Baghdad whose young minds were only beginning to develop? If so, how could any of them sleep at night? How could a single one of them call himself "Christian"? I agreed with the Psalmist: God would judge America, the "daughter of Babylon." The only trouble was that America is my home.

We who read the psalms, Dietrich Bonhoeffer advised, must read them as the prayers of Jesus. What could Jesus have meant when he prayed Psalm 137, blessing the one who dashes Babylon's children against the rocks? Perhaps the "children" of America were her bombs and missiles, tanks and aircraft carriers. Could it be that these "children," dashed against the rocks, might be the swords that Isaiah envisioned beat into plowshares? Then again, I thought, the "children" of Babylon's daughter might be her great ideals of "democracy" and "capitalism," "liberty" and "human rights." Could it be that those "children," so often worshiped as gods, were now being revealed for what they truly are—human ideas that, when worshiped, inevitably become diabolical? These "spiritual" readings of the text were helpful. I was no longer praying for the damnation of the pilots flying above me. But I remembered the wisdom of St. Thomas Aquinas who said that a more literal reading of Scripture, when possible, is to be preferred. And so it occurred to me: "*I am a child of America. I cannot* deny that *I* am a product of the daughter of Babylon. And I, beneath these bombs, am being 'dashed against the rocks.' But if Psalm 137 is a prayer of Jesus, then I can believe that he is with me. And though we may die together beneath these bombs, God will raise us up into a new humanity. With the new eyes that God can only give me here, I may be able to see a new way forward for America. If I am born again in Babylon, I may be able to proclaim a new hope to her. Since God's judgment is his justice and his justice is his love, I can pray Psalm 137, even though it be against me, and still put my hope in God."

The bomb that spurred these thoughts had hit close. So far as I could tell, it had not hit our building. But it could easily have been across the street. Within minutes everyone was up. We met briefly to make a decision together about what we would do. Our instructions from the Iraqi Foreign Ministry for that day were to meet a representative at Al Fanar Hotel, command-central for IPT, and be escorted from there to bomb sites. In our discernment over the past few days, however, we had begun to see our mission as "first-response" prayer and action. The Iraqi government was trying to keep a firm grip on us. They did not want us going anywhere they didn't approve of beforehand or seeing anything they didn't want us to see. What were they hiding from us? We weren't sure, but we knew that we couldn't speak so firmly against the injustice of our own government while kowtowing to Saddam's tyrannical regime. We decided we would leave our hotel without permission and go find where the bomb had hit. We tried to call our friends at Al Fanar to tell them where we'd be, but the phone lines were not working.

I could see the smoke cloud rising when we walked out the front door, behind some buildings and down a bit, close to a large traffic circle. It was a few blocks' walk to ground zero of the explosion. We passed an Iraqi traffic officer on the way and asked him where the bomb had hit. He nodded down a street to his left and pointed us in the direction of a communications center that was still smoldering. We could now see why the phone had not worked at the hotel. All communications in our district of the city had been knocked out with a single blow.

Across the street from the communications center we saw an older gentleman standing outside a small hotel. He was visibly disturbed. "Look at this! Look at this!" He said to us. The blast from the explosion had shattered every window on the front side of his hotel. He invited us inside to see the damage. Fragments of glass were strewn across the floor, and tables were overturned in the lobby. We climbed the stairs to the second floor, and the man pointed to a pallet on the floor where he had slept the night before. With dramatic hand motions and broken English, he described to us how the blast had wakened him with a shower of glass pouring across the floor. He had been so frightened that he urinated all over himself. Somewhat embarrassed, he pointed to a wet spot on his pallet.

Listening to the old man's story, I saw him motion to a young man, his son, as he continued describing the scene from earlier that morning. His son ran downstairs and quickly returned with a case full of Pepsi. He was sorry he could not do more, the old man told us, but he wanted us to know that we were welcome here. In the ruins of a little hotel where we had come to mourn, a party broke out. We thanked them for the drinks and asked about their family. They asked where we were from and how we liked Iraqi food. The hospitality we had already come to appreciate during our few days in Iraq was transforming a destroyed place into a center for new relationships, new community. We were laughing together by the time we returned to the street. The old man asked us to take some pictures of the damage his building had suffered. Cliff Kindy, a member of the permanent CPT team, turned his back to the street to video the broken windows across the front of the hotel. As he did so, I saw an Iraqi police car pull up behind him.

A couple of officers approached us and asked the old man a question in Arabic. He looked concerned and started speaking very quickly, pointing at us and at his hotel. A number of us pulled out the little sheets of paper we carried with us that described in Arabic what we were doing in Baghdad. One of the officers read a copy, looked at us, and handed it back. He wanted us to go back into the hotel. In the lobby he asked the old man more questions. He was particularly concerned about Cliff's video camera, it seemed. Cliff rewound the tape to show him what he had videotaped. He was only documenting damage in the hotel, he explained. He had not turned the camera toward the bomb site across the street. The officer was not satisfied. As we worked to communicate with one another through a translator, another car pulled up. Officers from that car got out and came into the lobby. They indicated that we should all follow them and get into the cars. We were being arrested by the Iraqi police.

I made sure that Leah and I got into the same car. Though the officers seemed calm, we still had no idea where they were taking us or for what purpose. I had read reports in the United States about political prisoners in Iraq and the torture tactics Saddam's men used on those who questioned his authority. These officers didn't seem nearly so sinister as the images those reports had evoked. But how would I know what a torturer looked like? I prayed silently as we rode through the streets of Baghdad: "Lord, we are in your hands."

When the cars stopped, the officers ushered us very respectfully into a police station. Down a hallway to the left I could see dark cells with bars across the front, much like the ones I'd seen at Alcatraz when I visited San Francisco once. An Iraqi man sat huddled in the corner of one, his head between his knees. We, however, turned down a hallway to the right and were ushered into an office. The officers made sure each of us had a chair to sit in. One by one, they asked our names and ages, recording them by hand in a notebook. They asked if any of us were hungry and brought pita bread in from another room. One officer dumped some figs on a table and welcomed us to take what we would like. If these were the same men who did Saddam's dirty work, they sure were nice about it.

We did not know how long we would be there, so after we had given the officers all the information they wanted, we started to sing. We sang about Paul and Silas, remembering the early church and those who went to jail for the sake of the gospel. "We shall overcome," we sang, remembering civil rights leaders in America who had gone to jail for the sake of justice in the sixties. Peggy taught us the words to sing "We are not afraid," in Arabic. She had learned them from an Iraqi boy whom she'd gotten to know in Baghdad. As the officers listened, we sang. And when we stopped, they asked us to sing some more. One officer picked up a ruler and waved it in the air as if he were conducting an orchestra. Our song was a welcome sound in their ears. "How can we sing the songs of Zion while in a foreign land?" the people of God ask in Psalm 137. We can sing them when we realize that no land is foreign, so long as God is there. Any Babylon can be redeemed if we will remember Zion. The kingdom of God can even break out in an Iraqi jail if we believe. Miracles do happen.

Between songs I asked the group to share stories of miracles they had witnessed in their lives. Weldon Nisly shared about praying with Christians in Russia for a nonviolent end to Communism and then watching it happen as the Berlin Wall fell just days after he'd returned home. Cliff Kindy told us the story of a drug lord whom he'd confronted on the street in a little town in Colombia. Weeks later he learned that the man had become a Christian and asked a pastor to help him get out of the drug cartel. In the midst of our uncertainty, I was encouraged by these stories of God doing things I could hardly believe. In some of their darkest moments, my teammates testified, light had shone through. Though the future was uncertain, we had reason to hope. The God who works miracles was with us in that Iraqi jail. He would be with us whatever happened.

Then Mr. Sayd, our Foreign Ministry liaison, stormed in the door. "What are you doing here?" he scolded. We began to explain, but he was not interested. "Give me your cameras. All of you. You have made a big mistake." He took all of our photography equipment and left the room. In a few minutes he returned. "OK, let's go," he said. "I've had you released but you must leave the country now." Mr. Sayd escorted us to Al Fanar, where the other members of our team were waiting anxiously to learn what had happed to us. With all communications down, it had been impossible for us to call them from the police station. Sis Levin gave us a big hug. "I thought it was Beirut all over again," she said with a sigh of relief, referring to the day Jerry had been kidnapped by the Hezbollah in Beirut, Lebanon. The team was relieved, but some of them were not happy. What were we thinking, going off on our own, breaking the rules, and not telling anyone? We could have been killed for all they knew. And now we had to deal with the Iraqi government deporting us. Would the whole peace team have to leave?

Kathy Kelly exhibited extreme patience as so much that she had worked for with Voices in the Wilderness and IPT looked like it was crumbling. "When do those who were arrested have to leave?" she asked Mr. Sayd. "Immediately," he said sternly. "They must leave now." "But that would mean they would have to drive through the desert at night," Kathy said slowly. "Couldn't they wait until morning to leave?" Mr. Sayd softened. "OK. They will leave first thing in the morning." With that, the decision was made. We would have to leave Baghdad five days after we had arrived, coming and going again before the U.S. troops ever made it to the city. We would have to leave part of the team that had shown us how the new humanity is possible even in the harshest of realities. We would have to leave the Iraqi people who had welcomed us so warmly and thus expanded the borders of our beloved community. And, worst of all perhaps, we would have to sojourn once again through the desert. "I'd rather be in the street when the tanks get here than on that road tomorrow," Leah said. But on that road again was where we would be, by order of the Iraqi government. Without knowing it, they were opening a door for us. Once again, it was the Spirit driving us into the desert. Off the highway, in the little town of Rutba, God wanted to show us a new way toward peace. He would use the Iraqi government to get us there, just as he'd used the decisions of the U.S. government to bring us to Iraq. The King of kings was still lord of the universe, even though the road ahead looked perilous. We went to bed one last time by the waters of Babylon and slept more soundly than we had since arriving in Baghdad.

V.

WHAT HAPPENED IN RUTBA

C PT met for devotions at 8:00 a.m. the next morning. Jim Douglass, who had not been arrested and would not be leaving with us, began our time together with a prayer from Thomas Merton:

> My Lord God, I have no idea where I am going. I do not see the road ahead of me. I cannot know for certain where it will end. Nor do I really know myself, and the fact that I think I am following your will does not mean that I am actually doing so. But I believe that the desire to please you does in fact please you. And I hope I have that desire in all that I am doing. I hope that I will never do anything apart from that desire. And I know that if I do this you will lead me by the right road though I may know nothing about it. Therefore I will trust you always though I may seem to be lost in the shadow of death. I will not fear, for you are ever with me, and you will never leave me to face my perils alone.

On the road to Baghdad, Jim said he had prayed this prayer of abandonment to God. He talked to us about his friendship with Thomas Merton when he was living and how "Tom" had taught him to see the world differently. Jim spoke with a quiet confidence about the God that he and Tom worshiped—a God whom we could trust far more than we can trust ourselves. The road that lay before us was uncertain, Jim said. We could not know what awaited us in the desert. Would we encounter U.S. troops again? Would the bombers overhead mistake us for combatants? Would we make it to Amman? We could not know the answers. But we could know that God is with us. We could be sure that the team in Baghdad was praying for us. And we could be confident, Jim said, that Tom was also interceding on our behalf as a member of the eternal communion of saints. We would not be traveling alone.

After we had prayed together, we all descended the hotel stairs to the lobby, where our friends would bid us farewell. As I wound my way down, I thought about Jim, who was walking behind me, and how much Leah and I had valued his presence on our journey through the desert to Baghdad. I turned and asked, "Jim, will you be my Thomas Merton?" Jim stopped walking, squinted his eyes, and thought carefully. "Well, let's see," he said. "You could ask me, and I could ask Tom, and Tom could ask God...." He smiled an "Aha" smile with his eyes. "Yes, I think that would work."

Three cars had been hired by the Iraqi government (at our expense) to carry us out of Iraq. One was a large GMC; the other two were yellow taxicabs. Our caravan was already parked in front of the hotel by the time we got down to the lobby. We packed up some bread and water for the road and walked out to the curb. Those of us who had been arrested were joined by an Irish journalist and a Korean man, who were both being deported for other reasons. Our friend, Shane, from Philadelphia, had also asked to leave with us. With the rules tightening more and more in Baghdad, he felt like he could do more by telling people in America what was happening in Baghdad than he could by staying. We hugged our friends good-bye. In his classic newsman style, Jerry smiled and quipped, "Like our great philosopher Yogi Berra said, 'It's déjà vu all over again!'" He gave us a bear hug. Jim was waiting by the curb to say good-bye to us. We hugged. Looking into our uncertain eyes, he smiled and said, "It's going to be a wonderful day."

Leah and I got in the front car with the Irish journalist, Peggy Gish, Kara from our delegation, and Betty Scholten, another member of CPT's permanent team in Iraq. Our driver was a small, round man who looked very serious. He had been hired by the Iraqi government to get us out of his country. He meant business. Mr. Sayd walked over to the car to give us his send-off. He had told Leah on the sidewalk that we could have our camera back for two hundred dollars. "Don't worry," she had told him. "It's not worth that. You can keep it." After giving instructions to the driver in Arabic, he reached his hand through the window and put our camera in Leah's hand. "I hope you will have a safe trip to Amman and be able to come back to Iraq someday— under different circumstances." He looked us in the eyes, and he meant what he said. The explosion of anger at the police station the day before had been partly an outburst of frustration, partly a show to assure the police officers that he was in control. Iraq was, as Cathy had told us, a "control society." But Mr. Sayd was a human being. He felt bad for us as we drove away, and he was vulnerable enough to let us see it.

The sun was shining in Baghdad as we pulled away from Al Fanar. The oil fires that were still burning painted single lines of black across a clear blue sky, not stopping to hover over the city. I could see so much more than I'd been able to on our drive in. There were a few checkpoints on the outskirts of Baghdad where Iraqi soldiers waved us through without any question. Our driver stopped once to talk to a man at a gas station, about the road we assumed. There didn't seem to be any problems. On the sides of the road farmers and shepherds were out in their fields. We passed a couple of trucks that were going into the city. After an hour of driving, our eyes were peeled for the hill on which we had seen the U.S. troops, no more than one hundred miles outside of Baghdad. When we finally spotted it, there were no troops. Only sand, as far as we could see. The charred frame of the militiamen's vehicle still sat by the roadside.

The first place we stopped for gas had been abandoned. There was no one there. We got back on the highway and continued driving. At another rest stop, one where we had stopped on our way in, we tried once more to get gas. Again, no one was there. The building was locked and the pumps were turned off. Had the drivers not thought about this before leaving Baghdad? I looked at the gas gauge and saw that we had less than a quarter of a tank. There was no turning back. The farther we traveled, though, the more removed we were from civilization. Had the Spirit driven us out into the desert to stay? I wondered how long we might last with the bit of bread that we'd picked up in the hotel lobby on our way out.

As our gas gauge dipped toward empty we spotted another station ahead. Like the others, it was closed. Whoever usually sat out here in the middle of nowhere to run these pumps had left. They had locked the doors and taken their keys with them. We were stuck. Our drivers were standing around, presumably talking about what to do, when a white van full of Somalian students pulled up. They asked in Arabic about the situation and then told us in English not to worry. They would take care of the pumps. One of them popped the hood of their van and pulled the battery out. He carried it with him behind the gas station. After a few minutes he came back, saying the pumps should work now. I was amazed. "How did you know how to do that," I asked the young man. "Oh, where we come from this is very normal," he said. "We must do it all the time." I thanked God that before this man had come to study at the university in Baghdad, he'd had a few lessons in the practical necessities of life in a war zone.

Not long after leaving the gas station, we passed by the little town of Rutba, through which we had made our detour on the way in. Staying on the highway, we saw that, indeed, the bridge for eastbound traffic had been bombed. Traffic going west, however, could still pass through on a part of the bridge that had not been hit. Our driver slowed down considerably as we passed by the broken concrete and twisted steel on the other side of the bridge. Just beyond Rutba, off in the distance on the left side of the road, we saw a cloud of dust rise from a bomb that had just been dropped. My eyes scanned the sky for the sight of an airplane, but could not find one. Five minutes later we passed an anti-aircraft artillery piece that had been shot up and burnt out. Clearly we were in the midst of fighting. But no one was in sight. Then, ahead of us on the other side of the road, we saw two tanks. Were they American or Iraqi? Was it just the two of them, or were there more behind? Our driver slowed as we watched closely to see what would happen. Leah reached into her bag and pulled out a white towel to wave as soon as she saw a human face. But there was none. The tanks had been bombed from the air and were abandoned.

As we approached the turnoff to go to the Jordanian border, I breathed a sigh of relief. Though we'd had a few scares and traveled at a breakneck pace for four and a half hours, we were safe now. Our driver pulled to the side of the road to wait for the other two cars to catch up with us. We saw a yellow taxi in the distance and were relieved. Two cars accounted for. Only one to go. But the third car did not come. We asked the driver of the second car when he had last seen them, and he said it was sometime before passing Rutba. The longer we waited, the more we began to think that something must have gone wrong. Finally, we saw a car coming. It was the white van of Somalian students we had met at the gas station. "We have seen one of your cars turned upside-down on the side of the road," they said to us. "Was it bombed?" we asked. Some of them motioned as if a missile had come out of the sky and hit the car. Another who spoke English, however, said he did not think it was a bomb. "There was blood in the car, but the doors were locked and no one was there." Whatever had happened, someone had been conscious enough to lock the doors.

We told our driver that we had to go back, but he refused. We could not go back. Going back was not an option. He would take us to the border and check on our friends on his way back to Baghdad that evening. But we had to go back now, we insisted. We would not leave our friends for dead in the middle of a desert. Back and forth we made our case to one another as we stood outside the vehicles in the middle of the highway. Our driver would not budge. The driver of the second car, however, seemed sympathetic. It occurred to me that the third taxi driver might be a friend of his. So I turned my pleas in his direction. Once he was convinced, he worked with us to convince our driver. Finally, he relented. Motioning his hand for us to get back in the car, he climbed into the driver's seat and turned the GMC around. We would go back to find the third car.

It took us more than twenty minutes to get back to where the car was. All the way, we were silent, each of us praying as we stared at the road. "God, please let them be alive," I thought. "Oh God, please let them be alive." Cliff, Weldon, and Shane had all been in that car, along with the Korean man and the Iraqi driver. I thought about the prospect of finding them dead on the roadside. But if they weren't there, where were they? Had someone taken them away? Where to? How were we ever going to find them?

We found the car empty with blood on the seats and splattered across the windshield. Someone's head had left a spiderweb crack in the glass. The car was on its side in a drainage ditch at the bottom of a hill, not five miles from Rutba. The left rear tire had a hole in it, and from the looks of the marks that the car had cut into the highway, we surmised that it had blown the tire while traveling very fast before careening to a halt when it went off the road into the ditch. That impact, no doubt, had thrown the passenger into the windshield. His injuries, at least, were probably serious.

Because the accident had happened so close to Rutba, we assumed that our friends had somehow made it into town. Indeed, that was the case. Even as bombs were falling to the left and right of the road, some Iraqis had stopped and taken three injured Americans into their car. When they arrived in Rutba, they were taken to a doctor at a clinic who spoke to them in perfect English. "Three days ago your country bombed our hospital," he said. "But we will take care of you because Muslim or Christian, Iraqi or American, we take care of everyone." He sewed up both Cliff and Weldon's heads, saving their lives. Weldon had been the one in the front passenger's seat whose head hit the windshield. His injuries were indeed the most serious. He had broken numerous bones and most likely had internal injuries also. The doctor did all he could to bind Weldon's wounds and ease his pain. He also put Shane's right arm, which was probably broken, in a makeshift sling.

When we drove into town we stopped to ask for directions to the hospital. "There is no hospital," a man on the street corner told us. "The Americans bombed our hospital." He pointed us to a clinic, where he said we might find our friends. When we arrived, Shane was standing outside, waving to us with his good arm. I was so happy to see him that I started laughing at his lanky frame on the horizon, one hand strapped against his chest, the other waving in the air. It was so good to see him alive. "Everyone is OK," Shane said as we jumped out of the GMC. "They've taken wonderful care of us here. Everyone is OK."

We went inside the clinic where Weldon and Cliff were both lying on beds. The doctor greeted us and began describing what he had been able to do for our friends. "Thank you so much," I said to him. Weldon, the doctor told us, would need to get to a hospital as soon as possible. Immediately, I started trying to lay out a plan of action. I had noticed a Red Crescent ambulance beside the building on the way in. "May we take our friend to the border in your ambulance?" I asked. "It will be bombed," the doctor said matter-of-factly. His response sounded unreasonable, but then I remembered seeing an ambulance bombed out on the side of the road. This man did not trust the planes overhead. Three days before, they had bombed his hospital. "Then we'll have to lay him across the seat in the GMC," I said.

A number of men helped us carry Weldon's bed to the GMC, which was parked outside. As we talked about the best way to get him onto the seat without hurting him, I noticed a man holding his hand above Weldon's face, shading him from the sun. He was a strange looking man, dressed in a long, white robe, unlike the Western dress that most Iraqi men wore. His hair was reddish and his eyes a striking blue. I didn't think much of him at the time; I just noticed that he stood out. After we had placed Weldon on the seat as gingerly as possible, though, I noticed the same man again, now on the other side of the car by Weldon's head. Leah was sitting on the floorboard beside Weldon and had closed the door carefully, protecting his head. Suddenly, the strange man in the white robe opened the door again, bent over, and kissed Weldon on the forehead. Then he closed the door softly and walked away.

Weldon later told me that up until the time we took him outside the clinic, he had not seen the man in white. He was neither part of the clinic staff nor one of the people in the car that had stopped to pick them up on the roadside. Weldon, however, distinctly remembers him shading his eyes and kissing him on the forehead. He remembers his white robe and his blue eyes. Had I not seen the man myself and only knew Weldon's description of him, I would tend to think he was the product of a hallucination. Weldon was, after all, on the verge of going into shock. What he saw, though, I also remember seeing. In the hustle of an emergency situation, when I didn't even remember to ask the doctor's name, the man in a white robe stuck out to me. Where had he come from?

As we were leaving Rutba, we asked the doctor what we owed him for his help. "Nothing," he replied. "You owe me nothing. Please just tell the world what happened in Rutba." What *had* happened in Rutba? Some strangers had stopped to help their injured enemy, even as bombs were still falling. It was a Good Samaritan story. At the same time, the Iraqi driver charged with deporting us had turned his car around and brought us back to Rutba. It was a miracle. A doctor who spoke perfect English had done everything in his power to care for our friends. And, finally, a stranger—an angel, perhaps?—had kissed Weldon on the forehead and assured him that everything would be alright. What had happened in Rutba? Something incredible, though I was certain I had not begun to understand it.

We drove quickly, without incident, to the Jordanian border. On the Iraqi side Weldon got out of the car and sat up for a few minutes in the waiting area. He was not doing well, as the Iraqi officials could see. They hurried us through the paperwork and sent us on our way. At the Jordanian border office, our Iraqi drivers dropped us off and turned to drive back to Rutba, where they had left the third driver, who'd also been injured. We asked immediately for an ambulance to take Weldon to Amman. As we sat in the waiting area, Weldon grew very pale and passed out at one point. A medical student on-site came to give him an IV. After some time, an ambulance arrived with another doctor. I helped Weldon to the ambulance and stayed to ride with him to Amman. The rest of the team would take a bus from the Organization for International Migration (OIM) to the refugee camp for registration and then on to Amman.

As we set out for Amman it was already dark. I asked Weldon how he was doing, and he flashed a great big smile. But he was grimacing also. I knew he needed to get to a hospital fast. So I was glad, at first, that the ambulance driver was moving quickly. Soon, though, I began to worry that he might be driving a little too fast. Every curve in the road pulled at my stomach. I could only imagine what it was doing to

Weldon's aching bones. And the engine sounded like it was doing five thousand rpm's. I prayed that we wouldn't blow a tire like the taxi had outside Rutba and relive the same scene again on this side of the border. Then I heard the engine blow. We coasted to the side of the road and stopped. The driver pulled out his cell phone and called for another ambulance. This one was going nowhere.

When a second ambulance came after about thirty minutes, its driver insisted on moving Weldon from the bed of the first ambulance to the bed of the second. For some reason it was important to keep each bed with its ambulance. Weldon moaned as we rolled him up off of one bed and down onto the other. Still, when I asked him how he was doing, he smiled. When we had set out again, I remember thinking to myself, "what else could possibly go wrong?" Not very long after that, the tire on our second ambulance went flat. The driver did not lose control, but I did begin to lose composure. This was beginning to feel like a dark, dark comedy. I tried to laugh, but I couldn't. Crazy as it was, it just wasn't funny. Weldon, I began to worry, might not make it.

The third ambulance, however, got us to the hospital. It had been, I figured, almost twelve hours since the accident. When the doors of the ambulance opened, a bed was there to rush Weldon into the emergency room of the best hospital in Amman. I was surprised to hear a woman ask if I was Jonathan Wilson-Hartgrove. "Yes," I said. "And where is Leah?" she asked. I told her that Leah was on a bus, headed to Al Monzer hotel in Amman. But how did she know my name and that I was married to Leah? She was a representative from the U.S. Embassy, she told me.

Weldon was stabilized in the emergency room and admitted to the hospital. The doctor said Weldon's body had had it pretty rough, but he was going to be OK. I left him there and rode with the Embassy representative to Al Monzer, where Leah and the others had already been back for hours. It was 4:00 a.m. Jamil greeted me at the desk with a hug and gave me a key to our room. I felt like I had come home. I walked upstairs, gave Leah a brief report, lay down, and went to sleep.

A few hours later I woke up to a beehive of activity at Al Monzer. The United Nations had reported in its morning press briefing that we were the first international observers to confirm rumors that a hospital had been bombed in Rutba. Every major news network in the world had set up a bureau in Amman. All of them wanted to hear what had happened in Rutba. For the next two days, then, we told the story nonstop. Reporter after reporter came by Al Monzer to get the details about what we had seen. We told them the story about how the Iraqis had picked up our teammates and carried them to Rutba. We told them about the doctor who had saved Cliff's and Weldon's lives. We told them about our opposition to the war and our witness for peace.

When CNN learned that American civilians had come out of Baghdad during Operation Iraqi Freedom, they called us in Amman to request an interview. Leah and I had decided to fly home the next day, along with Shane and Cliff. Leah, Shane, and I agreed to meet a driver at JFK in New York. He would take us to CNN's studio to record a spot for the next morning's show with Paula Zahn. Though we were, by that time, eager to get home to Philadelphia, we also wanted to fulfill the doctor's request and tell the story of Rutba to as wide an audience as possible. While members of our team had talked to the BBC, South African News, a paper from Tokyo, and Germany's ZDF, we still wanted Americans to hear about Iraqis who were opposed to our war against them but still wonderfully gracious to Americans in need. When CNN called back for a preinterview, Shane eagerly told a research assistant about the doctor who had said, "Three days ago your country bombed our hospital. But we will take care of you because Muslim or Christian, Iraqi or American, we take care of everyone."

Shane paused as the voice on the other end of the line asked a question. "No, they were definitely against the war," I heard him say. He twisted his face in a look of confusion. After hanging up, Shane explained that the research assistant was going to talk to her producer and get back with us about the interview. "What we're hearing is that the Iraqi people are really in favor of this war for liberation, but they just can't say so because Saddam is still in power," she'd told Shane. That wasn't what we'd heard or seen.

CNN did call back to let us know that the Jessica Lynch story had broken and they would have to get back to us about the Rutba story.

We never heard from them again. Apparently the military raid of an Iraqi hospital to save an Army private made for better news than the heroic rescue of three American civilians by the enemy in a town where the hospital had been a target. It was April Fools' Day, 2003. Though I could see plenty of irony in the situation, I had a hard time laughing.

Our return from Iraq was the beginning of a crash course in how the media works in America. What had happened with CNN was no strange conspiracy. It was a window into the news business, which chooses very carefully the stories Americans get to hear about what is happening in the rest of the world. That the United States did not hear the story of Rutba in the midst of Operation Iraqi Freedom has much more to do with who we are as a people than it does with any particular news outlet. Our media cannot tell the truth about people in other places, I began to see, because we cannot tell the truth about our own addictions to comfort and complicity. We hear those who praise the American Way. But we do not realize that the way we have been living for some time is killing us. Farmer and essayist Wendell Berry is extremely perceptive here: "It is wrong to suppose that we can exploit and impoverish the poorer countries, while arming them and instructing them in the newest means of war, and then reasonably expect to be peaceable." To consume endlessly without any attempt to care generously for poor and hurting human beings is a recipe for disaster. One need not be a seer to say so. As Jesus said, we need only to look at the "signs of the time."

What was most deeply troubling to me was the way in which the church in America had found itself unable to resist an unjust war precisely because we were so dependent on the economic domination system that had produced this war. (My dad told me that while we were in Iraq, someone at my home church suggested selling "United We Stand" and "Support Our Troops" bumper stickers as a fund raiser for the youth group.) Nearly every major denomination in the United States had made an official statement against a preemptive attack on Iraq based upon their understandings of just war theory and the global political situation. Yet, the church had still sent tens of thousands of young Christians to fight a war we had already condemned. Why?

Because the churches had not been able to see any alternative. It was easy to say that this war was wrong. Almost no one, however, had the resources to articulate clearly what would be right. Operation Iraqi Freedom had laid bare a frightening lack of moral vision in our churches.

On the flight to New York from Amman, we discussed the possibility of arrest at immigration. We had traveled to Baghdad in open violation of the U.S.-backed economic sanctions against Iraq. We knew that both fines and imprisonment were possible consequences. But it was important, we thought, to be as honest as possible. I looked at the space on the immigration form that asked, "What countries have you visited since leaving the United States?" and wrote, "Jordan and Iraq." Because we didn't know what would happen, I wrote a brief statement of our convictions that Leah, Shane, and Cliff approved. We gave it to some friends who were with us on the flight and asked them to put it in a press release if we were detained. We had our plan worked out by the time the plane touched down at JFK.

When we made it to the immigration booth, Shane was in front. He handed the officer his passport and explained that we had traveled to Iraq against the orders of our government because we thought those orders were unjust. If the officer agreed with the law, Shane said, we understood that he needed to arrest us. If he felt that the sanctions and the war were unjust, however, we invited him to ignore the law with us. "Oh, you're some of those crazy people who were over there with that Voices in the Wilderness," he said to us. "I know about you. I saw you on TV the other night." I wondered what the TV had said. "Let me talk to my commanding officer." We stood and waited as he walked to a back room and closed the door. In a couple of minutes he returned. "Well, you're alive," he said. "Welcome back to the United States of America." With that he stamped our passports and waved us through. Though the sanctions had been held against the Iraqi people for some thirteen years, they were evidently not worth enforcing against U.S. citizens.

We had never expected to be back so soon. Leah and I had left our jobs after conversations with our bosses in which they said they commended our courage but couldn't guarantee that they could hold our positions until we returned. We had left our last semester of classes at

Eastern, not sure if we'd return in time to graduate. We had on more than one occasion had to consider seriously whether we would ever make it back alive. Now, two weeks after we had left our home, we were back again. Because our flight was late and we were scheduled for a press conference in Philadelphia, we rented a car and drove south from New York. All along highway 95 we saw the billboards urging passersby to have pride in America and honoring the soldiers who were fighting for freedom. We listened to the radio reports from embedded media sources and asked ourselves whether they were really in the same country we had just left. What they were seeing was so different from what we had seen. But surely they weren't lying. As we listened, it occurred to me that they were simply seeing a different reality. Embedded behind the U.S. guns, they could not see the Iraq we had seen. The only Iraqi eyes they saw were eyes that focused on the tanks and Hummers, machine guns and armored cars that were the instruments of their death. What the embedded reporters saw was all that America could see. No wonder so many people were behind this war.

Though we had a lot of things we had left hanging at home that needed our attention (like the jobs that our employers graciously invited us to return to and the papers we had to make up if we were going to graduate), Leah and I committed ourselves to telling as many people as would listen what we had seen in Iraq. (For Leah this was a huge commitment; she hates speaking publicly.) Local news stations wanted to do interviews. The *Philadelphia Inquirer*'s Jim O'Niel, who had covered our story very faithfully since we left, wanted to do a follow-up piece. Eastern wanted us to speak on campus. Pastors invited us to their churches. Magazines wanted to run the story. And the local peace groups wanted a report. To all of these people we tried simply to say what we had seen and heard. The experience was often frustrating. TV stations would cut and paste our statements into sound bites, distorting the point we were trying to make. We got mail from people who were angry: how could we condone the evil Saddam Hussein had committed against his own people? Did we not respect the soldiers who were giving their lives for our country? And why did we hate America? That's what a lot of people wanted to know.

I was hurt that so many heard hate in our words. We weren't hippies spitting at soldiers as they got off the planes from Vietnam. We weren't protestors screaming epithets about the President and the Man. We were trying to talk about God's love. In some settings, that was worse than our so-called liberal agenda. One reporter said to me as we were talking before we went on the air, "Now try not to get carried away with the God-talk. Keep it practical for our listeners." Religious language rang hollow with so many. Perhaps they felt like they had heard all of the rhetoric before. What difference did faith make in reality, though? That's what so many people really wanted to hear.

TV and radio spots, we began to realize, were not very effective ways to communicate truthfully with people. Sound bites seemed to encourage stereotypes. So we let the answering machine tell us if it was a TV station calling. And we stopped calling them back. Much more encouraging were the in-depth interviews with good, honest journalists and face-to-face conversations where we got to hear what people were thinking and respond to them. We read a letter in response to one of Jim O'Neil's articles. "When I heard George W. Bush say that he was an evangelical Christian, I vowed to myself that I could never be one," she wrote. "But when I read Jonathan and Leah Wilson-Hartgrove's story, I thought, 'Maybe I should think again about Jesus and Christianity.'" Those were the sorts of responses that kept me going.

When we spoke to the community at Eastern, we told some stories about what we had seen and heard and then opened ourselves to questions. Though it wasn't the easiest thing for us, it was good to hear people's reactions—somewhat subdued, perhaps, by the academic setting—and to grapple with the difficult questions they raised. How were Americans supposed to know the truth about what was happening in Iraq if we couldn't trust the media? Did we think working to vote Bush out of the White House would be a good next step? Had we been able to communicate our Christian motivations to Muslim people in the Middle East? What would we have said if we had run into our classmate who was serving with the Marines in Iraq? They were the kinds of questions that we needed to be wrestling with. I didn't have all the answers, but I felt much better about a setting where we could talk about them honestly.

The Institute for Global Engagement was kind enough to publish an interview in which they asked me all of their critical questions about our trip. The political climate of this Christian think tank where I had been working for over a year was fairly conservative. Though they recognized the complexity of the global situation, they were certainly in favor of the U.S. going to war against Iraq. Still, they did not silence me. They offered a space in which I could explain myself. My boss, Chris Hickey, asked the questions that represented IGE's reaction. "Isn't it naïve to think that you can go off as a well-to-do American, traipse through the desert, show up without really knowing anything about the country, and think you'll make a difference?" No one had said it quite so bluntly, but I knew that, behind their courtesy, lots of people were thinking the same thing. "I think it would have been naïve if we thought we could stop the war," I said.

It *was* "foolish" in the way that I believe God calls us to be foolish—to proclaim the kingdom of God in the midst of a world that doesn't really believe the kingdom is possible because it's not what we see in the politics of the world. So I'm not going to argue with folks who say, "That's a crazy thing to do." I mean, I agree. If you only believe in the political realities we see on the news, it is crazy. But we believe in a kingdom that is more powerful than the U.S. government—and certainly more loving. So we wanted to proclaim that kingdom to the people in Iraq and, more importantly, perhaps, to people here, people who know us better than the Iraqis know us.

But wasn't the way we chose to speak our message a stunt of sorts? Christians, Chris reminded me, are called to humility—to do things in secret that only our Father in heaven can see. What did I have to say to those who thought we had put on a show at a lot of other people's expense? I thought carefully before responding.

Was it a stunt? Well, if a stunt is something done to draw attention to the people doing it, then no. But was it an intentionally public act that was meant to draw attention to

91

something? Yeah. We intentionally stepped into a global conflict because we wanted to draw attention to Jesus's way of nonviolence in the world. So, in that sense, it was a symbolic act—the sort of thing I see Jesus doing all the time when I read the gospels. You know, if you ride a donkey from the Mount of Olives down into Jerusalem, you're doing a "stunt" in a very real sense.

Chris followed each of my responses with another question on the list. Had the media attention we'd received gone to our head? Might there not have been a better time for a peace delegation to Iraq? What about the unintended consequences of our actions—the taxi drivers' lives we had unnecessarily endangered? Was it really good stewardship to risk our own young lives? Hadn't Iraqi government restrictions limited our ministry to civilians? Were we not—by implication—standing with a tyrant who had gassed thousands of his own people? How did we as Christians justify breaking U.S. law? After each question, Chris paused to let me respond.

I weighed my words carefully as he recorded what would be my most lengthy public response to the hard questions that most people were afraid to ask. I was grateful for this opportunity. Chris concluded by quoting one of the sound bites I'd used on TV when reporters asked what it was we were trying to say with our actions. "That Jesus is Lord and America is not," I had said time and again. "I think it makes for good press, and I think it's true," Chris said. But he wanted to know if the distinction were not too simple. Must Jesus and America always be opposed to one another? "Isn't it possible," he asked, "that in this situation the U.S. may, even though acting out of self-interest, also be advancing the sorts of things God would approve of?" He was referring to democracy, religious freedom, and human rights—all the things we worked for at IGE. Chris wanted an answer to the question of faith and politics that I had been asking ever since I was a Senate Page in Washington, DC.

Is it possible that God is using this situation? Sure. God's ways are well beyond our understanding. Throughout history God has used the sins of nations to carry out his purposes. So I think it very well may be that the United States is sinning *and* that God will use it. However, is it possible that this war is something God wants his people to be part of? I don't think so, because I think we have to look at the question through the lens of Jesus—God's revelation to us about how human beings should live in the world. "Here's an example: God's going to come and be a human being. Look at him. See how he lives." And when we look at Jesus we see that he rejects the temptation in the wilderness to have economic, political, and religious power. He turns aside from all those things to follow the way of the cross to Jerusalem and suffer nonviolently for the sake of the liberation of the whole world. I mean, Jesus liberated the whole world without a single bomb. Why can't his church be faithful to that example today?

Still, I do think it is important to recognize that, as you noted I've said before, "Jesus is Lord and America is not." I think there *is* a clear dichotomy there on the level of lordship. America should never be lord. Jesus is Lord. It doesn't mean that America is terrible. I mean, all kinds of really good things shouldn't be lord. My possessions shouldn't be lord. My wife—great person—but she shouldn't be lord of my life. And I shouldn't worship her. So when I say that Jesus is Lord and America is not, I'm simply trying to remind American Christians, who I think are particularly tempted to worship the idols of our nation, that we're called to follow Jesus. We're called to be citizens of the kingdom of God. And there's nothing better than that. There's nothing better for us as individuals, and there's nothing better for the United States of America.

I did not hate America. Yes, I was critical. But my criticism was rooted in love, just as Chris's respectful presentation of the difficult questions our trip raised was a manifestation of IGE's love for me. What I wanted was an honest presentation of what was happening in the world and the good news Jesus had to offer all of us. The mainstream media had not let us say to America what had happened in Rutba. But the hospitality we had received there, I sensed, was key to envisioning Jesus's third way here in the heart of Babylon. The excitement I felt as I remembered our short time in Iraq reminded me that I had been born again in that land of ancient Babylon. Could I, however, get born again *again* in the Babylon that is America? The question was whether I could find the strength to love my own country as much as the people in Rutba had loved us. With me, it was impossible. But with God, all things are possible. It was time to move beyond Baghdad.

VI.
REBUILDING IN THE RUINS

Six weeks after our return from Baghdad, Leah and I graduated from Eastern. It was a wonderful weekend. Both sets of our parents came to Philadelphia to celebrate our finishing college and, more important to them, surviving our trip to Iraq. My dad told us how he had gone through a spiritual crisis while we were in Baghdad. Late one night, as he was praying in bed, God had spoken to him and given him peace. "It's like I have a new relationship with Jesus," he told us. My mom described her own experience in prayer. She found herself still praying for the people of Iraq, the burden of their suffering now heavy on her heart. Leah's dad shared with us the impact our trip had had on his students and others around the country. And Leah's mom, who had managed our e-mail communication during the trip, gave us a two-inch stack of messages that people had sent her in response to our reports. We shared stories, ate good meals, and laughed with one another. The whole weekend felt like one big, long sigh of relief.

After it was over, Leah and I had to face a question: would we return to Iraq with the Christian Peacemaker Teams or stay in the United States? CPT had offered to put us through training and bring us on full-time with their organization. I had also been offered a scholarship to study at Duke Divinity School. Should we go back to Baghdad or on to Durham, North Carolina? We couldn't imagine a life better than the one we had known in Amman and Baghdad. Of course, life as full-time peacemakers would not be easy. But full-time peacemaking was now part of what it meant for us to be Christians. We would be doing it wherever we went. The question was one of location: should we leave America again to return to Iraq or should we work on following Jesus and proclaiming his peace at home? We decided the challenge of living faithfully in the American church was the one God was calling us to face. We would do it in Durham, an old tobacco city in my home state.

Since returning from Iraq, Leah and I had received scores of letters and e-mails from all over the country, each representing a small pocket of resistance and witness. Though many of these people weren't anti-war protestors, they implicitly recognized that our journey to Iraq was connected to the church's work of hospitality—particularly its care for the poor and neglected in America's inner cities and impoverished rural communities. These people were seeing the same thing CNN had seen, only from the other side: hospitality is subversive to the powers that make war possible. In her book *Making Room*, theologian Christine Pohl makes the point this way:

> Although we often think of hospitality as a tame and pleasant practice, Christian hospitality has always had a subversive, countercultural dimension. "Hospitality is resistance," as one person from the Catholic Worker observed. Especially when the larger society dishonors certain persons, small acts of respect and welcome are potent far beyond themselves.

Just as important as our actions against war, we were beginning to see, were our intentional and systemic efforts to be for hospitality. The two are inseparable. Only in resisting what Eisenhower called the military/industrial complex can we love our neighbor in the world today. Only in loving our neighbor can we discover the little way to resist such a powerful system. To act as the body of Christ in the world is to love God by resisting the destruction of his image in the victims of war and embracing that same image in the poor among us. To love

God, Jesus said, is to love your neighbor as yourself.

We knew a little bit about houses of hospitality from people like our friend Shane, who lived at The Simple Way community in Philadelphia. Leah and I had spent a good deal of time there during our college years, learning about Dorothy Day and the Catholic Worker Movement. In the dark days of the Great Depression, Day had heard the call of peasant philosopher Peter Maurin to start a newspaper proclaiming the social teaching of the Catholic Church and the importance of the traditional works of mercy. When people in need read about the hospitality and love of the church, they came to Day asking where they could find it. "Here," she said, opening her door to the poor. Inspired by Day's story, hundreds of houses like The Simple Way have sprung up in cities around the world. Jim Douglass, whom we respected deeply after our time with him in Iraq, also lived at a Catholic Worker house of hospitality in Birmingham, Alabama. We talked to people we knew to see if there was such a house in Durham. Catholic Worker houses had been established south of Raleigh and in Chatham County, both about an hour away. But no one knew of anything in Durham. Could we start a house? We traveled to Birmingham to ask Jim what he thought.

"A Mennonite Worker?" Jim said to us. "Sounds like a great idea!" Jim considers himself more a "Catholic shirker" than Catholic Worker because he spends most of his time writing. He referred us to his wife, Shelley, for all of our practical, how-to questions. The most important thing we needed was a community of like-minded people. Running a hospitality house by ourselves would be difficult, especially with me studying and working in churches while Leah tried to make a living. We sent out an e-mail to people in the Durham area and others we knew would be moving there. Would anyone like to help us start a house of hospitality? Isaac Villegas said yes.

Isaac had been one of Leah's dad's students at Westmont College in Santa Barbara. The son of immigrants from South America, Isaac was interested in the "base communities" that had given rise to the church-based liberation movement in Latin America. He had seriously considered moving to South America to join one of these communities. But he sensed God calling him to study theology at Duke.

A house of hospitality, he thought, might be a "base community" from which he could find a way of liberation in the North American context. Though we lived on opposite coasts, our understanding of the church in North America was almost the same as Isaac's. It was no coincidence that both he and I had been attracted to Duke.

Stanley Hauerwas, one of Duke's theological ethicists, had said in a sentence what I'd begun to suspect was true: "God is killing Protestantism in America, and we deserve it." Hauerwas knew as well as I did that it is not only the Mainline Protestant church that is falling apart in America. Perhaps he was more comfortable saying such damning things about a denomination he was himself a part of. But the church as a whole—Catholic, Mainline, and evangelical alike—had been "democratized" into consent by the powers that be in America. Each individual was free to worship her personal Savior only so long as she served the State in all things political. To bridge that divide was simply against the rules of American Christianity, it seemed.

The American church's response to the war in Iraq had only been one manifestation of a deep flaw in our thinking about what it means to be the body of Christ. In his book *Living Faithfully in a Fragmented World*, Leah's dad, Jonathan Wilson, asserts that both the church and the culture at large are experiencing a crisis of fragmentation. We in the West cannot conceive of what it would mean to be faithful to Jesus Christ because we have inherited only pieces of the practices that would allow us to live our true vocation. Though we still confess, "Jesus is Lord," we often don't have any idea what it means politically or economically, in our marriages or in our jobs. Like Hauerwas's damning critique, Jonathan's assessment is rather bleak. But there is hope. In a book entitled *After Virtue*, Notre Dame philosopher Alasdair MacIntyre argues that most of the virtues we know today survived the Dark Ages in small, disciplined monastic communities that lived by the rule of St. Benedict. "What matters at this stage," he wrote, "is the construction of local forms of community within which . . . the moral life can be sustained through the new dark ages which are already upon us . . . We are not waiting for a Godot, but for another—doubtless very different—St. Benedict."

For the church, Jonathan says in *Living Faithfully*, there is even more reason for an expectant hope. "We can look with greater hope than MacIntyre expresses in *After Virtue* because we look to the power of God through the gospel to renew faithful living and witness." The power we look to is the very same power that raised Jesus from the dead. Hauerwas may be right that God is killing the church in America—killing all the parts of us that are stubbornly unfaithful. But, as St. Francis said, "it is in dying that we are born to eternal life." God is able to raise up from the ruins of Christendom a church that follows the way of Jesus. If Jonathan and MacIntyre are right, it occurred to me, then God may be revitalizing the church through a new monasticism.

Monasticism, theologian Walter Capps says, is the West's "most enduring and powerful form of counterculture." So as we started our hospitality house in Durham, I began to read about the history of monastic movements in my studies at Duke. I looked at the long sweep of church history and began to see that Capps is right: the church's response to compromise and crisis has consistently been one of new monastic movements. When Constantine made Christianity legal and offered the favors of his empire in the fourth century, the Desert Fathers began the first monastic movement by fleeing the centers of power and creating alternative communities in the desert. In the midst of the Crusades, as religious violence raged, St. Francis rejected economic privilege and started a new monastic movement. Not all monastic movements had been within the Roman Catholic communion, though. The Anabaptists of the sixteenth century had sought to establish a community of authentic Christian witness over and against the corrupt state churches of Europe. Likewise, slaves in the United States cultivated a liberation theology and tradition of subversive song in the underground churches of Christian plantations. In an age when Christian America had become the "last remaining superpower" and declared an all-out "war on terror," it seemed to me that once again it was time for a new monasticism.

The more we thought about and tried to practice a new monasticism, the more we realized that location matters. Neo-monastic movements seemed to grow out of the places that the Empire ignored—wildernesses and wastelands; slave quarters and urban ghettoes. We had already begun to develop a relationship with such a place in Durham. When we had asked locals where the problems were in Durham, they had pointed us to Walltown. A low income African-American neighborhood, Walltown had become a center for drug trade in the 1980s and, more recently, for the gangs and violence that followed. Churches in the neighborhood had come together in the late 1990s to start Walltown Neighborhood Ministries, a center for community organizing and social ministry. Leah had started volunteering there shortly after we arrived in Durham. The director, Rev. Sylvia Hayes, was excited about our idea of a hospitality house and said she could refer people who were in need of shelter to us. We had our first guest by the end of the week.

Already up and running, we needed a name to call ourselves. But none of us had any good ideas. We decided we would wait until a good name came along. While talking to Jim Douglass on the phone one evening, I mentioned our need for a name. He promised to think about it. The next day there was a message on our answering machine: "Hi, this is Jim Douglass calling to suggest that you name the house 'Rutba'. Those people were wonderful at hospitality." While we knew some folks might have a hard time pronouncing the name when they saw it, the prospect of people asking "what's Rutba?" seemed like an open opportunity to continue our doctor friend's request that we "tell the world what happened at Rutba." I recorded a new message for our machine: "Hi, you've reached the Rutba House. Please leave a message." Jim had helped us make the connection between Iraq and Durham.

We had talked as a community about Leah's vocation in Durham. Walltown Neighborhood Ministries seemed like just the sort of work she wanted, but it was only volunteer work. There was no money available. My stipend from Duke wasn't enough for us to live on. And it would be hard to offer hospitality if we couldn't eat ourselves. But if God wanted Leah in Walltown, we reasoned, he could make a way out of no way. We decided she would keep volunteering at the Ministries' office and we would all pray for money to come. It was a little experiment in the economics of providence. The next week Rev. Hayes told us that two part-time positions had become available and she'd like to hire Leah. We were delighted. God had opened a way into Walltown.

We started worshiping at the St. John's Missionary Baptist Church in the heart of Walltown. Though we were the only white people in the room, the congregation made us feel welcome from the start. It took a while for us to get used to the worship style. I could sing, and I could clap, and I could sway, but I had a hard time doing all three at the same time. Still, I loved the music. I enjoyed the heartfelt prayer. And, most of all, I loved the way in which all my political stereotypes got mixed up in the black church. In every evangelical church I had ever been a part of, conservative theology meant right-wing politics. More liberally minded people usually wobbled on basic doctrine. At St. John's, though, a conservative theology mixed well with more liberal social convictions. Most folks there loved Jesus with all their heart *and* thought the war in Iraq was a bad idea. I didn't agree with everything I heard, but I certainly appreciated the fact that I didn't always hear what I had come to expect. The world looked different from Walltown.

So we decided we needed to move. The house we had rented not too far away from Walltown was already full. So we needed more space. More than that, though, we needed to move into Walltown, across the "Broad Street divide" that separated white and black, safe and dangerous in Durham. The only trouble was that most of the houses in Walltown had two bedrooms or less. All the bigger houses had been split up into duplexes. Then, one day, Leah spotted a big old house with a "For Rent" sign in the front yard. The owner was fixing it up himself and "just wanted to make sure that whoever rented it would put it to good use." It was adjacent to St. John's property and had five bedrooms and a large common space where we could have community meals. The Rutba House had found a place in Walltown.

At the Rutba House, I have found my place. Together with people who love me, I am experimenting in the truth of a new monasticism. Not all of our experiments have been successful. Actually, we mess up a lot. That I live in a community where mistakes do not mean disaster, though, is a testament to me that something good is happening. Forgiveness is possible. By God's grace, we are able, on our good days, to speak truth to one another, to hear the truth about ourselves, and to still know that we are loved. That is a gift from God.

More importantly, we are not alone. New monastic communities are scattered all around the country, seeking to live faithfully in the way of Jesus. Most of them have been at it for much longer than we have. Just this past year we started a "community of communities" network in which we are talking about the new monasticism as a movement of God's Spirit in the North American church today. We are learning from one another how to shape a rule for life in our communities, much like the old monastic orders lived by a rule. We're building a network of mutual support that we hope will give birth to new communities, offering guidance and wisdom to a culture that is increasingly hungry for an alternative. At our first "School for Conversion" in June of 2004, we discussed and agreed to the following statement of marks that characterize our neo-monastic communities:

Twelve Marks of a New Monasticism

Moved by God's Spirit in this time called America to assemble at St. John's Baptist Church in Durham, North Carolina, we wish to acknowledge a movement of radical rebirth, grounded in God's love and drawing on the rich tradition of Christian practices that have long formed disciples in the simple Way of Christ. This contemporary school for conversion which we have called a "new monasticism," is producing a grassroots ecumenism and a prophetic witness within the North American church which is diverse in form, but characterized by the following marks:

1) Humble submission to Christ's body, the church.
2) Relocation to the abandoned places of Empire.
3) Geographical proximity to community members who share a common rule of life.
4) Hospitality to the stranger.
5) Nurturing common life among members of intentional community.
6) Sharing economic resources with fellow community members and the needy among us.
7) Peacemaking in the midst of violence and conflict resolution

JONATHAN WILSON-HARTGROVE

within communities along the lines of Matthew 18.

8) Lament for racial divisions within the church and our communities combined with the active pursuit of a just reconciliation.
9) Care for the plot of God's earth given to us along with support of our local economies.
10) Support for celibate singles alongside monogamous married couples and their children.
11) Intentional formation in the way of Christ and the rule of the community along the lines of the old novitiate.
12) Commitment to a disciplined contemplative life.

May God give us grace by the power of the Holy Spirit to discern rules for living that will help us embody these marks in our local contexts as signs of Christ's kingdom for the sake of God's world.

In our life at Rutba House and in conversation with other neomonastic communities, I am beginning to see how my conversion in the Middle East prepared me to get born again *again* on American soil. The beloved community of the new humanity that Jim helped me to see in Amman is something I continue to experience at the Rutba House. There is nothing magical about our life, of course. We share chores and economic resources. We eat and pray and read the Bible together. We throw parties and have fun. The community doesn't seem quite so beloved to me when the sink is full of dishes and everyone else has gone to bed. Our life is not without its problems. But with a little work and a lot of grace, we're able to live peaceably together—black and white, male and female, married and single. In a neighborhood where the breakdown of the nuclear family is almost total, we live together as a different kind of family that defies almost everyone's stereotypes. Who is my mother, my sister, my brother? Together we are asking Jesus's question again. "Whoever does the will of my Father," Jesus answered. We're seeking to discern his will as a community.

In the desert I learned that we often cannot hear God unless we have learned to abandon ourselves to him in contemplation. In our culture of conspicuous consumption, we have asked ourselves at the

Rutba House what practices might equip us for contemplation. While the Christian tradition provides us with enough options to fill another book (a book which I would very much like to write), the practice we have chosen to do together is fasting. After dinner every Thursday, we covenant with one another not to eat again until Friday at dinner (unless someone is sick or traveling or feels like it would be rude to turn down an invitation to lunch; we're actually quite flexible). In my experience, nothing is more spiritually jolting than the conscious decision to deny myself the food my body needs. When I do, my body cries out, "Why have you forsaken me?" In a small way, I must face the darkness. For an American who rarely thinks of death, "the last enemy to be defeated," this is an important practice. I can't imagine being willing to give my life to Jesus if I don't even have the self-restraint to forego my daily bread.

We also have a prayer nook under the stairs at the Rutba House where I try to meditate in silence every morning. I'm not very good at it. My mind races from one thing to the next as I try to breathe deeply and contemplate the cross before me. Beside the cross there is an icon of Phil Berrigan with nuclear flames surrounding him. Phil spent a good portion of his adult life as a priest in prison for resisting America's nuclear program. He reminds me of the new monastics who find their prayer cells in prisons around the country. Below the icon of Phil is a picture of Mother Teresa. She holds a rosary in her hand, the crucifix close to her lips. She is kissing Jesus, her Lover, whom she loved back in the disguise of the poor. I hope that she is praying for our houses of hospitality now. In this quiet place, as I focus on the cross, I contemplate the faces of those who pass through our life at the Rutba House. In the busyness of "helping," I so often fail to see our guests for who they are: Christ come to visit me. In the prayer nook I write poems to say what I cannot otherwise find words to speak. Poems like this one:

Ecce Homo
"Shit," he grumbles,
Then swings his legs
Into the elevator
And slumps onto his walker.

Second floor is district court
Where paupers go for begging
Without an orange vest.
D.A. asks his name
And he says, "Bobby,
My name's Bobby."
"Last name, Sir...
Aw, what's the charge?"
I hand him the ticket.
"Can't believe they send me these,"
He says while spinning 'round
On an Italian leather sole.
Through twisted smile and squinted eyes:
"I'll have to pull a Pilate here
And wash my hands of this man."
Bobby's beard is sticking out
Because his chin's held tight.
Not a word for his accuser;
Behold, the human being.

At Rutba House we try to practice the radical hospitality we received from the people of Rutba and Baghdad. In a city as racialized as any in the South, we open our doors to the poor and create a space where middle-class white folks like me can share life with our African-American and Hispanic neighbors, whom we might otherwise never get to know. At Rutba House we're learning how hospitality is peacemaking in a city riddled with the violence of gangs, poverty, and segregation.

One of the things we've learned from other friends in the new monasticism is how friendship with the poor offers a different kind of security. There's a lot of talk these days about security for the world, for our homeland, and for our children. I can't imagine a neighborhood any less secure than Kensington, Philadelphia, where The Simple Way is located. When our friends decided to move there five years ago, they could hardly get the real estate agent to show them a house in the neighborhood. It's the poorest district in the state of Pennsylvania. Just down the block from the house they eventually bought, at the intersection of Kensington and Allegheny Streets, more heroin is sold on a given day than anywhere else in the nation. It's the sort of neighborhood that your mother taught you to lock your doors when you drive through. For five years now, The Simple Way has been inviting people off the streets into their home and taking meals from their kitchen to share with people on the streets. Often people ask them, "Don't you feel unsafe here?" I love their answer: "When you're friends with the people on the street, you don't have to feel unsafe."

Hospitality offers a different kind of security. But just as terrorists can slip through a ballistic missile shield, the security of friendship isn't perfect. Hospitality doesn't produce immunity from the violence of this world. It can, however, transform it. In the fall of 2003, after we had returned from Iraq, our friend Shane was walking to the post office in the middle of the day when two men jumped him from behind and knocked him to the ground. Immediately the guys on the corner shouted, "You've got the wrong man!" And the two men ran away. Shane, however, was left with a broken jaw. As it turns out, he was no more safe on that particular day than the people who live in fear of his neighborhood. The difference, I think, is that he still loves the men who jumped him enough to pray for them. Jesus said, "Love drives out fear." Because Shane chose to love his enemies before they ever harmed him, he can still live in peace in Kensington.

The friendships that are made possible by hospitality not only create a different kind of security. They also teach us to see the world differently. Roy, a fellow who lives with us at the Rutba House, has been opening my eyes to the structural violence of our town. I came to Durham to study because I think Duke Divinity School has one of the best theological faculties in the world. Roy has lived in Durham his whole life. He calls Duke the plantation. Whatever I might learn at Duke, I cannot forget that it is for Roy a symbol of the white establishment that excludes poor blacks, caters to its own self-interest, and pays low wages to the minorities who keep it running. White folks like me, who benefit from the power structures of this society, cannot see what Roy sees. He is teaching me what Dietrich Bonhoeffer called the "view from below"—a vantage point Bonhoeffer was privy to only after his imprisonment at Tegel by the national security state. With Roy's help, I am learning to tell the truth about myself. Seeing things I couldn't see before, I'm trying to find concrete ways to repent of the social evils in which I am complicit.

"Repent," Jesus said, "for the kingdom of God is near." What we learn from hospitality is not only that the present order must pass away, but that a new world is possible. When we practice Christian hospitality, we invite others to share in God's peace. We have some friends in the new monasticism network who've started a hospitality house in the Waterfront South community of Camden, New Jersey. They're the first people to move into Waterfront South in years. Because of rezoning and redlining after the second World War, Waterfront South has become a textbook case for environmental racism. Within a two-mile radius, there is a cement factory, a sewage treatment plant, a trash-to-steam incinerator, multiple scrap metal yards, and government designated superfund sites to store radioactive waste. In the middle of all this, there is a struggling neighborhood. Our friends moved in, looked around, and decided one of the things they had to reclaim was the biblical mandate to "till the earth and keep it." So on the little piece of earth that was theirs, they took an old refrigerator, laid it on its back, and made it into a compost bin. They planted impatiens in old toilets and set them in the back yard. They tilled up the driveway to plant a vegetable garden and hung a hammock in the tree. Pretty soon, an urban garden surrounded the newly christened "Camden House."

Our friend Chris told me a story about a fellow named Steve, whom he met on the street in his neighborhood. For years Steve has been living in abandoned houses. He lamented to Chris how terrible his life has been—on and off drugs, abandoned by friends, without dignity. Chris didn't really know what he could do for Steve, so he just invited him to sit in the garden. There Chris listened as Steve talked. The next day, Steve came back. Chris got him a glass of water, and they sat and talked again. The next day, Steve came back again. And he's been coming ever since. "The other day," Chris told me, "Steve looked at me and said he doesn't feel like he's in Camden anymore when he comes over to our place. He says our garden makes him feel at peace."

Hospitality, we are learning, is about inviting people in little ways to share in God's peace.

Exploring the possibility of a new monasticism within the United States, I am finding ways to live out my conversions to the politics of Jesus in beloved community, to contemplation as a center for action, and to hospitality as peacemaking. Beyond Baghdad I am finding that God is still calling, leading me forward into the unknown. Could a new monasticism really be the hope of the church in North America? Is the Spirit calling us, as he called St. Francis, to "rebuild my church which is in ruins," by establishing outposts of God's love in the abandoned places of Empire? While we have said that this monasticism needs to be for the whole people of God, not only for those with religious vocations, I don't dream of every Christian in America joining an intentional community in an urban center or moving to a farm in Appalachia. This is not the only way. But it is a way that is needed, I think. I do dream of a church in which new monastic communities would make sense. I dream of congregations that would support houses of hospitality, as the Chapel Hill Mennonite Fellowship supports us at the Rutba House, both spiritually and financially. I dream of more farms like the Silk Hope Catholic Worker, where homeless people from the cities can go to "till the earth and keep it" while they get back on their feet. I dream of more communities like the Bruderhof where our friends find ways to provide meaningful work for every member and take good care of their children and the elderly. I dream of more churches like Christ Community Church in Des Moines, Iowa, where eighty percent of the congregation is part of a house church in which individuals covenant to hold one another accountable to their commitment to confess Christ as Lord in every facet of their lives. I do dream of a network of established communities to which the church could point when people ask, "What does the alternative way that Jesus offers look like?" I dream of a church that could say, "Come and see!"

But is the new monasticism really an answer to the problem of war? Does this life we are trying to live have anything to say to those in Washington who have the power both to start wars and to end them? Can anyone really believe that it might be possible to overcome the power of the Pentagon? Again, I must quote Jim Douglass—this time from his book, *Lightning East to West*:

> The Pentagon's power comes from the grip of an illusion, our own egos. The force of truth and love lived in their depths is a force of unity, of life itself. That force is real. We need to join in a community committed to that nonviolent life-force which is the power of the powerless. We need to test the truth by betting our lives on it in the world. If a community can experiment deeply enough in a nonviolent life-force, the power of the Pentagon will crumble.

I can believe this only because I have seen that another way is possible. Though the world may kill us in our attempt to love it, God will raise us from the dead. The power that we know in the cross is indeed enough to end the violence of the Pentagon. But not by destroying it. The end of history that we confess is one in which every knee shall bow and every tongue confess that Jesus Christ is Lord. The power of the Pentagon will crumble when we all bow the knee and confess that the Lord of the universe is a Lamb who was slain to set the whole world free, thus putting the lie to our myth of redemptive violence and wars of liberation.

Is it not naïve to think that soldiers and politicians would voluntarily lay down their arms and vow to "study war no more"? It is, only so long as the church is not willing to totally abandon itself to the humility (and power) of the cross. "The war continues," poet and activist Daniel Berrigan writes, "because the waging of war is total / but the waging of peace is partial." Violence is "necessary" because we who confess the cross have for too long failed to proclaim and practice it among the nations.

The church must have, John Yoder said, a "witness to the State." We should believe that the gospel is good news, even to those who are in power. But our witness must not be a veiled attempt to seize the State's power. The church cannot become a lobby for the Democrats or the Republicans. Nor should we be a base for grassroots movements organizing to secure power for the oppressed. To all of these groups we may be called to give a witness. But our hope is the kingdom of God. The only violence we know is the violence of love, which chooses to suffer with those who are suffering. The only power we believe in is the power of the cross.

"So you're a pacifist?" people ask me now. Usually I answer yes, though only reluctantly. My reticence is rooted in a growing conviction that the category of pacifism is not sufficient to describe the vocation of the church in America today. When it was suggested to Dorothy Day that she should be called a saint, she asked that the church not dismiss her so easily. My feelings are much the same with regard to pacifism. As a position, it is far too easy to dismiss. We in the church can no longer limit peacemaking to the vocation of nuns and priests or the historical peace churches. Neither can we confine it to the private or religious spheres. As citizens of the world's last remaining superpower in an age of increasing violence, American Christians have a responsibility to rethink our categories for moral engagement with our nation's enemies. We cannot debate "just war" and "pacifism" as equally legitimate options without recognizing that the categories make a distinction that left us with no faithful course of action to follow together in the spring of 2003. Just warriors told us that a war with Iraq would be unjust; pacifists said what they always say: no war is just. But neither camp was able to show us a viable alternative for the whole people of God. Compassion requires us to ask how we might lovingly resist violence in an increasingly violent world. This question drives us forward. My prayer is that it might also bring us together.

Since returning from Iraq, I've had the opportunity to talk with both pacifists and just war advocates about what it means to follow Jesus as Americans in this peculiar moment of history. I'm encouraged by those conversations, and they have shaped my thoughts in this small book while at the same time pushing me beyond Baghdad and these pages. I cannot conclude with any sense of integrity without saying that this work is incomplete. In the sense that it has been a personal work—an effort to say what our experience has meant to me—it is not finished because I am not finished. I have glimpsed the love of God, but I do not fully embody it. I have seen the promised land, but I do not live there—not much of the time, at least. There is an aching within me that repeats those lines from Robert Frost over and over again:

But I have promises to keep
And miles to go before I sleep,
And miles to go before I sleep.

In a broader sense, I recognize that this book and our experiences fit into a master plan of which I am only one small part. The vision I have is limited, and even what I see is not a dream that belongs to me. It is, I hope, a faithful witness to the work that God is doing in the world and to the end toward which we are being led. That end is always beyond us, though already in and among us. We pray, "Thy kingdom come," even as we hear Christ's words, "The kingdom of God is within you." We pray for our Lord's return while welcoming him in the poor and hungry. Acknowledging our own poverty and hunger, we see that he is us.

That the church is the body of Christ makes all of us uncomfortable, because we hope for more than we know ourselves to be. If what we see is the totality of Christ's body, there is little hope for the church. But if we are not Christ's body in some real and tangible way, there is no hope for the world. We must see clearly that the existence of God's whole creation is inextricably linked to the mystery of our existence as church in the nonviolent way of Jesus. As Martin King said so well, our options are no longer violence and nonviolence; we must choose nonviolence or nonexistence.

Not long after we returned from Iraq, I had the chance to view a screening of Martin Doblmeier's documentary, *Bonhoeffer*. Watching the story of Dietrich Bonhoeffer's resistance to Nazism prior to and during World War II, I was struck by the tragedy of the German church's silence in that dark night of the twentieth century. Though the Confessing Church did separate itself from the complicit Reich Church as an act of resistance against Hitler's regime, Bonhoeffer knew as we do now that their resistance to the evil powers behind Nazism was not thoroughgoing enough. "Only those who stand with the Jews can sing Gregorian chant," Bonhoeffer wrote from prison. There are times when a failure to stand with those who are suffering is a denial of Christ. Unfortunately, the steady chant of those who overcome by weakness was nearly a solo in Germany during its age of rampant nationalism.

The United States is not Nazi Germany, and I do not mean to suggest that our leaders are guilty of systematic genocidal hatred in the case of Iraq. The devil is far too clever to repeat a scheme about which we have all said "never again." But that does not mean that the powers of evil are not at work in the structures of our world today. The irrational nature of our nationalism in response to Operation Iraqi Freedom makes me question our spiritual resources to resist the powers of violence. We must seriously ask ourselves if there are *any* conditions under which the church would be able to withdraw its support from our government's policy and actions. If not, we are never far from the church that cried, "Heil Hitler!"

America's response to Doblmeier's film does give me some reason for hope. In the months before, during, and following Operation Iraqi Freedom, *Bonhoeffer* was on an independent tour in scores of churches and synagogues throughout the United States. Though every major media poll suggested that a majority of Americans were in support of the bombing and occupation of Iraq, Doblmeier told me that the dissenting voices were not silenced in the congregations he visited. Everywhere he showed the movie, Bonhoeffer's story sparked critical dialogue about what faithfulness in wartime means.

My hope is that, in some small way, the stories I have told here will inspire a similar response. I pray that they will cause Christians to remember the Iraqis, to remember our place in history, and, perhaps, even to remember the saints. If the church is to be the hope of the world in this time called America, we must return to the stories of martyrs like Bonhoeffer, Martin Luther King, and Oscar Romero. Remembering their lives, we cannot help but think critically about how the forces of evil are wreaking havoc via the U.S. military and our client states in the world today. Remembering the martyrs, we take up their crosses. "If I die," Archbishop Oscar Romero said before his assassination in El Salvador, "I will rise again in the Salvadoran people." Will the martyrs throughout the ages who constitute the communion of saints rise again in us, the body of Christ today? If we are in Christ,